The Imprisonment of
African American Women

The Imprisonment of African American Women

Causes, Conditions, and Future Implications

by
CATHERINE FISHER COLLINS

McFarland & Company, Inc., Publishers
Jefferson, North Carolina, and London

British Library Cataloguing-in-Publication data are available

Library of Congress Cataloguing-in-Publication data are available

ISBN 0-7864-0263-6 (library binding: 55# alkaline paper) ∞

Manufactured in the United States of America

*McFarland & Company, Inc., Publishers
  Box 611, Jefferson, North Carolina 28640*

To my brother,
the late Herman Fisher, Jr.,
the world's greatest musician.
I miss you and I love you.

And to my husband,
the late Clyde Collins.

Contents

Figures

Tables

Acknowledgments

This book has been developing for three years. At times I felt I could not go on reading and writing about the horrifying situation in which African American women and children find themselves in this wonderful nation, which supports some at the expense of others. I would read, become depressed, and put my reading and writing aside only to be pulled out of a sound sleep by a deeper voice within that said, "This story of your people must be told."

There are so many to thank, but I must first begin with the Almighty. For I truly believe that the voice I heard was God's voice, telling me that I could and would finish this book. Thanks be to God.

The following people have enabled me to complete my project and my thanks go to all of them. To my two wonderful parents, who *never* spoke a racist word in my entire life, the late Herman Fisher, Sr., and Catherine Lynch Fisher, I love you. To my daughter, Laura Harris, and son, Clyde II, you are so special; how do I thank you for being my children? To my caring son-in-law, Kenneth, and my grandchildren, Crystal and Kenneth II, you know how I feel: thank you. To Fay, my sister, and David, my brother, I include hugs and kisses.

My colleagues at SUNY Empire State College were a real positive force. Their encouraging words always made me and my work feel so very special. I would like to thank Dr. Imani Fryar for wisdom. The late Governor Hugh Carey of New York State, made it possible in the 1970s for me to work on the Commission of Corrections, which opened the doors in order to learn about New York State prisons and other aspects of corrections. It was this experience that brought to light the plight of African American prisoners and provided the impetus to write the first entire book devoted to African American women prisoners.

Michael Bauden, former chief medical examiner of New York City, and Dr. Phyllis Harrison Ross, members of the Commission of Corrections Medical Review Board, shared their knowledge and expertise. Maxine Sellers, my professor at the State University of New York at Buffalo, encouraged me to research issues of women in more detail.

The professional and technical support provided by Connie Coles and Marvel Ross-Jones is far beyond a thank you. I hope they know how much their help made it possible for me to complete this book. To my Jack and Jill of America, Inc., mothers and my Links Buffalo chapter sisters, thank you.

And lastly, to everyone that I missed, please know that you are all very special in my life and this work.

Introduction

In 1923 the number of imprisoned African American females amounted to 48 percent of all women committed to penal institutions for the first six months of that year (Lekkerkerker, 1931, p. 199). For every 100,000 African American females, 428.6 were in prison. This statistic, when compared to white women prisoners in 1923 whose rate was 44.6 out of 100,000, is significant and alarming. What is even more startling and disturbing about these figures is that over the decades these numbers have not gotten any better for the African American female. For example, in 1982 there were 63 per 100,000 African American women in prison, while the figures for their white counterparts were 9 per 100,000 (Flowers, 1987).

This book does not totally focus on the glaring lack of literature that deals specifically with the overrepresentation of African American female offenders, but rather pulls together scarce, fragmented, and scattered information from throughout the many social sciences and scientific fields in an attempt to better understand how the criminal justice system has failed this segment of the population. This book also investigates the gaps that exist in the scarce body of literature and statistical data regarding African American female offenders.

Chapter 1 presents the historical development of the United States criminal justice system and how it was systematically designed to imprison African Americans. Chapter 2 presents various theories of why women commit crime. This chapter attempts, in a summary format, to present those theories that best reflect what is thought to be the criminality of African American women. Also presented is the 1992 resurgence of the biological-genetic theory of criminality. This chapter concludes with the author's "wheel of misfortune" for what she believes to be a more realistic and viable model for African

American female criminality. Chapter 3 depicts existing African American female statistical data from various governmental sources. These data clearly demonstrate the disparity that exists in arrest patterns of African American women when compared to their white counterparts. In addition, the author presents her 1992 survey data results of state and federal prisons that house females in order to amplify the apparent discrepancies that exist in the currently available data. Further, chapter 3 addresses the issue of why the data are presented in such a manner that they do not clearly and accurately present the true African American female prison population. Chapter 4 takes a close look at the crimes that African American women commit. It also reviews the data regarding death row inmates and incorporates the current arguments regarding racial bias in legislation. This chapter concludes with a look at the major employees in correctional services: white men. Chapter 5, supported by 1992 survey data, addresses the children of African American female prisoners and the effect that prison has on their lives. The chapter includes the services for women prisoners with children and the effect prison has on their families. Chapter 6 presents the deplorable health conditions of African American women prisoners. This disparity in health status is supported by statistical data and numerous diagrams. Chapter 7 presents prison alternatives to incarceration, and features a new program initiative, sponsored by a group of dedicated community volunteers. Presented in chapter 8 is an analysis of the Violent Crime Control Law Enforcement Act of 1994, or the Crime Bill, as it is popularly called. Chapter 9 focuses on the treatment of incarcerated women of color in foreign and Third World countries, including Canadian Aboriginal women, minorities in England, South African blacks, and incarcerated women in Pakistan. Chapter 10 takes a look at U.S. courts and their impact on African American offenders. Issues regarding appointive versus elective judgeships, and whether black male, as compared to white male, judges render harsher sentencing of African Americans are presented. The results of a survey of jurists attempts to look at those prisoner characteristics that might influence their sentencing decisions. After careful consideration of all the possible remedies to such serious crimes and how U.S. correctional officials might intervene with alternatives, chapter 11 makes eight recommendations. These recommendations are followed by rationales that the author feels are particularly relevant to conclude this work.

Chapter 1

History of the U.S. Penal System

It would be impossible to understand how any American bureaucratic system operates without first exploring its history. Therefore, a look back may better help us to determine the idiosyncrasies of its development and clarify why there is an overrepresentation of African American women prisoners in the entire U.S. criminal justice system. This chapter also takes a historical look at how European penal systems, particularly England's criminal justice system, influenced the establishment of the U.S. colonial penal system. Then we will trace, to the extent recorded by legal documents and other literature, the incarceration history of African American women.

Jails, Reformatories, Workhouses, State Farms, and the African American Female

Jails, as they developed in the American colonies, closely mirrored those established in England although the exact date of the first English established jail is not known. In 1166 A.D., Henry II through the assizes of Clarendon required that each sheriff in each country establish a jail. Most of those early jails were under the supervision of the sheriff, municipal or city governments, or religious groups (Moynahan and Stuart, 1978). The purpose of the these early jails was primarily to hold individuals until their trial. If they were found guilty they were "sanctioned via whipping, amputation, loss of sight and many other gory punishments" (p. 42). However, if the prisoners survived these ordeals they would be released. Of course, most of them did not. In the eleventh and fifteenth centuries most of the jails were located in cellars, towers, dungeons, and bridge abutments. Once these jails became operational, they were turned over to private persons to run. (This practice appears to be slowly returning, and will be discussed in further detail in later chapters.) These early entrepreneurs were more interested in collecting a fee from the prisoners (who begged or depended on their family for money) to cover costs of food and bedding rather than the welfare of the prisoners. By the sixteenth century English jails were in deplorable condition. For example, Moynahan and Stuart cite: "There was no separation or segregation of inmates; all were confined together. Housed in one place were men, women, children and among them the mentally and physically sick, serious offenders as well as petty offenders" (p. 43). These cited conditions eventually led to one of the first attempts to provide housing for the so-called "loose women." Initiated by Edward VI in 1553, who gave land and mansions to serve this population, the facilities were given the name "houses of corrections" and were different from early established jails. Under the control of Toran justices, the houses of corrections were established throughout England to provide industrial schools for the young women, refuge for the old and poor, and a place to punish and correct vagrants. It was the intent of these houses of correction to instill good citizenship through religious instruction. In most areas of England these facilities existed adjacent to the English jail (Robinson, 1922), a practice that is common today in some U.S. communities.

The workhouse was also established as part of the English penal system, but more specifically to provide jobs for the poor. This system was supported by individuals who donated materials for the able-bodied poor to produce an article (for example, clothing) that would then be sold as a source of income to be shared with the prisoner who produced the item. By the seventeenth century there were three basic incarceration facilities in England: the common jail, the house of corrections, and the workhouses. American history shows that many of the original European settlers were former prisoners (for example, prostitutes), which may have provided the impetus for the English tradition of penal and incarceration systems brought to the colonies by the settlers. As the colonial society developed, the prison rules then became closely related to the religious beliefs of the settlers and were strictly enforced when applied to women offenders, which is also common in today's criminal justice system. This supposed norm is further explained below.

Colonial Women

Women offenders and their incarceration were a factor during the colonial period. However, comparatively few in number (were incarcerated, mainly) those of the servant class (whites were servants or slaves in those early years), usually for petty violations of religious and secular laws (Rogers, 1922, p. 518). Charges against white women first appeared in colonial records in 1640, 1647, 1757, and 1794. Between 1636 and 1776 approximately 60 women were charged with being the sole (usually for prostitution) or joint violator of laws. Because white women's roles in the colonial era were shaped more by economic, social, and religious circumstances, they were not "relegated solely to the role of wife and mother, nor were they considered to be dependent and inferior" (Feinman, 1984, p. 12). Therefore, men and women were punished by the same methods, and it was not uncommon to see women publicly whipped or hung along with male prisoners (Freedman, 1981). This held true in all other cases, with the exception of where the rules were stringently applied to colonial women. Adultery was one such female behavior and most feared in the colonies "because the adulteress threatened familiar and secular stability ... of that time ... and was considered a dangerous person, and subject to punishment by both the church and the state, through excommunication and/or public humiliation" (Feinman, 1984, p. 13). The first penal institutions to be built in the colonies were jails and these were the places the few women offenders were held.

Slaves and the Colonial Penal System

As America became colonized, the rules of not only religious and secular beliefs but also of slavery—which had long been acceptable practices of the Europeans—were to be found in the colonial way of life. Those who established the colonies in this new world brought not only their personal possessions and skills but also their internalized social institutions as well; all of which left an awesome, indelible stamp on the penal system of later centuries. One of those indelible stamps was chattel slavery, an outgrowth of servitude by indenture. The indentured servant helped to fill the need of the colonists by providing free labor. These servants, who were white Europeans, were brought by boat and sold into servitude for a period of time ranging from four to seven years. The so-called labor contract was known as "indenture" (Sellin, 1976, p. 134). These white servant-slaves had the benefit, however, of freedom at the end of the contract, and because of their white skin it was very easy for them to assimilate into the white colonial society, something the black African slaves would not be able to do. These white servants paved the way for the first black slaves brought to Virginia in 1619 who were originally treated like indentured servants. But 21 years later the newly named "Negroes" who followed them became transformed into the property, real or personal, of their masters (Sellin, p. 134). Among these first 20 African slaves who arrived on a Dutch man-of-war were at least 3 females (Voices of Triumph, 1993, p. 28).

By 1830 there were nearly 2 million black slaves (Voices of Triumph, p. 31) working to build America's colonies. Records indicate that as early as 1640 in Maryland and Virginia blacks were being sold into a life of slavery. This system of chattel slavery became entrenched in the colonies and flourished especially in the South, where the tobacco, rice, sugar, and cotton planters found slave labor an invaluable, unequaled source of profit (Sellin, p. 134). This system was so profitable for the plantation owners that by 1790, with the first national census, Virginia had 292,627 slaves, South Carolina had 107,034 slaves, Maryland had 103,036 slaves, and North Carolina had 100,572 slaves. Out of the total Southern population of 12 million there were 4 million enslaved Africans (Voices of Triumph, p. 31).

Jailing of slaves was not profitable for the slave owners, so very few slaves were ever incarcerated for an extended period of time. Instead, prior to the Civil War, black slaves would be imprisoned in plantation-built jails and punished for crimes committed (for example, running away, stealing, assaulting an overseer, or disobeying an order) by the slave master who had unlimited power, including deadly force (Sellin, p. 134). Although in many states the plantation laws prevailed, the slave master (who dominated the courts) found it necessary to pass laws that were sanctioned in the "Negro Court." Punishments handed out in the Negro Court for crimes committed by slaves were not applicable to whites who committed the same crime (Sellin, p. 136). This practice is still evident in today's U.S. court system where a black female who steals $100 can receive six months in jail, while her white counterpart may receive a slap on the hand and be sent home to her family. Prior to the Civil War, when blacks were found in jails outside the plantation, they had already been subjected to the laws of the so-called Negro Court and were usually awaiting trial for felonies (for example, striking the master three times, which was punishable by death). On some occasions female runaway slaves would be found in jails (but rarely), usually waiting for their master to claim them. Unlike today,* imprisonment was unprofitable for the plantation owners because it deprived them of the benefit of free labor. So it was not until after the Civil War that large numbers were incarcerated.

Following the Civil War, Southern states found themselves lacking the manpower to rebuild large plantations and cities ravished by Yankee gunfire. To accommodate farming and city planning needs, Southern lawmakers once again crafted an incestuous plan by creating laws that would surely be broken by the multitude of hungry, and now homeless, former Southern slaves. For example, "the state of ... Missouri secured passage of ... the ... 'pig' law, which defined the theft of property worth more than $10,000—including cattle and swine—as grand larceny, punishable by five years of hard labor" (Adamson, 1983, p. 562).

Once these racist "Jim Crow" laws were broken by displaced homeless and hungry slaves, the Southern states found untapped legalized manpower. By the twentieth century these laws were replaced by unethical enforcement practices, the results being basically the same (for example, pro bono attorneys who are overworked and uninterested in the black women to whom they are assigned by the courts for representation, and plea bargaining where other prisoners are traded off). This new influx of black females constituted the largest number of women imprisoned under these laws. The black women were funneled into a new slave state program: "the so-called lease system, whereby, for a fixed per capita consideration to the state, prisoners were turned over to private employers, called lessees, who could work them at will" (Lekkerkerker, 1931, p. 66). This practice has been reinstituted in some states and will be discussed later.

These women were put to work on the large, decaying plantation cotton fields or assigned to mill work sewing in a large central building. This lease system was very profitable for the Southern states, but like any other unsupervised system there was much brutality and neglect. In some cases black women, once kept alive to bear children as property for the slave master, were either worked in the fields or sold. These black women were becoming a liability to the lessees, the new masters, who were held

---

Congress in 1996 appropriated $22 billion for prison beds (most contractors will be white) and created 100,000 new police officer positions (most of whom will be white men).

marginally accountable for these women's food, clothing, and medical care. In order to reduce their liability, in some cases these black prisoners would be literally worked to death (Rafter, 1985, p. 150).

According to the 1880 census record, Florida and Georgia leased all females; whereas Alabama, Louisiana, Mississippi, North Carolina, Tennessee, and Texas leased out some of their female prisoners and worked others in main plantation buildings. In states such as Tennessee, women were leased to work in mines and on railroads. Other female prisoners, who were chained to men,* would sometimes become pregnant. Once the black woman was pregnant she would be less productive, which prompted the expansion and building of more central buildings to imprison "dead heads": juveniles, black pregnant females, the aged, and the mentally ill. Seldom were white women imprisoned in these facilities. If white women were imprisoned, they were segregated from black females and assigned to more pleasant tasks. For example, in Florida white and black women were segregated in separate buildings with the laundry adjacent to the black women's quarters. In Georgia and Texas black women labored in the fields while white women sewed, gardened, and cared for chickens (Rafter, 1985, p. 152).

To assure that the Southern prisons would continue to have an abundance of free black labor, judges would refuse to send white women to prison and would often penalize black women more severely than white women. For example, "In the south after the Civil War ... blacks were arrested in large numbers and severely sanctioned for larcenies ... white women were seldom imprisoned for larceny" (Rafter, p. 146; also see chapter 10). Regardless of where these black women were imprisoned from 1865 until 1935, "as a rule, the higher the population of blacks in prison the lower the level of care, but white women were treated better than black women even in predominantly black penal institutions" (Rafter, p. 149). As the two separate penal systems developed—one for blacks and one for whites—white Americans found themselves with others (for example, children and the insane) who would also be segregated.

America's Segregated Jails and Reformatories

Early jails housed the insane, ill, aged, children, and hardened criminals, along with black women prisoners. All were confined to filthy

---

A system of chained gangs has recently been reinstituted in Alabama.

quarters where they, like the English prisoners, had to pay for their keep. However, in 1790 one of the first attempts to classify prisoners according to their crime or unfortunate state took place. The year 1790 was noteworthy in that blacks made up 12.1 percent of the American population. However, enslaved blacks had numbered 18 percent of the American population (and this figure has never been reached again, as cited by Hacker, 1992, p. 227). An outgrowth of this situation was that the Pennsylvania legislature authorized the renovation of the Walnut Street Jail, which brought about the separation of hardened offenders, removal of children entirely, and put women in a separate jail or building. The jails in which these women were incarcerated were referred to as workhouses or houses of detention. Available records show that these early jails contained work rooms where women were assigned the stereotypical female tasks of that era: making cigars and hoop skirts, weaving, sewing, and making silk hats (Klein, 1973). By 1820 it became apparent that the Walnut Street Jail population would eventually become problematic due to overcrowded conditions and the lack of a disciplinary system. Because most of the individuals who settled in the colonies had been former white prisoners in England, they did not believe in or institute harsh prison treatment. Instead, the authorities instituted a silent system* that was somewhat enforced by the architecture of the jails (LEAA, 1976).

In 1737 New York State, the front-runner in the prison industry (a distinction that still holds true in the twentieth century), added a new concept to the penal system by building an almshouse. The almshouse served as both a workhouse and a house of corrections for vagabonds, beggars, runaway slaves, and poor people refusing to work. Eventually, there was no distinction between almshouses, houses of corrections, or workhouses. All of these institutions started to look and operate like a jail. It was not until 1825 that prisons were built specifically to house women. Prior to that time women were confined to what many characterized as lenient houses of correction and local jails (Strickland, 1976). This new concept of separation led to the introduction of female matrons first in the Baltimore prison system.

By 1835 there were women's quarters in Alburn, Washington, and Witherfield prisons, with the first separate 90-cell structure for women built in New York at Sing Sing Prison (McKelvey, 1972, p. 36). In some states, however such as Massachusetts and Michigan, men and women

Prisons where inmates were not allowed to talk or speak to one another.

were still confined to the same workhouses. In other states, like Wisconsin and Illinois, the women's building and adjacent yard were within the walls of the state prison. However, they were not used for the intended purpose, but rather to ease overcrowding in male prisons. In addition to the overcrowding of New York's Sing Sing Prison, there were several prison scandals (women prisoners became pregnant while incarcerated), leading public supporters to urge the building of separate reformatories for women. These events helped to spark the controversy that led to the construction of reformatories for women in Indiana in 1873; followed by Massachusetts in 1877; New York State in 1887, 1893, and 1901; and New Jersey in 1913 (Lekkerkerker, 1931).

From their inception the first of these three reformatories housed primarily white women. For example, in 1910 New York and Massachusetts reformatory populations were approximately 95 percent white females, while Indiana recorded 72 percent (Freedman, 1981, p. 80). This racial bias in prisoner placement was allowed to exist by various "fuzzy" classification rules. In addition, such racial bias permeated other state systems, such as New Jersey, Ohio, and Pennsylvania reformatories, where black women were held in segregated, separate cottages. By 1930 the Illinois Reformatory operated four cottages for black women and four for white women. Between 1797 and 1801 in New York State 44 percent of the women sentenced were black. This state did not openly segregate black and white women prisoners. But in other prison systems black and white women were segregated because of a notion that "a peculiar attraction has been found to exist between 'colored' and white women in confinement which intensifies much danger, always present in an institution, of homosexual involvement" (Lekkerkerker, 1931, p. 234). Apparently, in New York State female prisons "black and white women lived together in the same cottages because Warden Katherine Davis refused to segregate the races" (Freedman, 1981, p. 139). There were, however, those in the New York State prison system administration who demanded that blacks and whites be segregated to prevent lesbian interracial sex. Using this homosexual argument "served as an excuse to segregate black women" (Freedman, p. 140).

As this early prison system emerged, black women were housed primarily in penitentiaries where there was no hope of rehabilitation, while white women were housed in reformatories where rehabilitation programs were the ultimate goal. In reformatories where most whites and very few blacks were confined, the common practice of the old

Figure 1.1 Females by Race and Sex in the Prison System

White Female 35.2%

Black Female 64.8%

Penitentiaries

Source: Prepared from Nichole Hahn Rafter, data: *Partial Justice: Instate Prisons 1800–1935*, p. 146, copyright 1985, Nicole Hahn Rafter. Used with permission of Northeastern University Press, Boston.

Southern plantation/lessee programs prevailed. Black women prisoners were assigned to the laundry while white women were given paid office jobs. In comparing the number of black and white females in penitentiaries and reformatories in 1923 the results of a now segregated system were apparent (see Figure 1.1).

The majority of prisons built between 1930 and 1966 were built with the reformatory model as the goal for young white women, while blacks were confined to arduous physical farm camps. In Strickland's 1966 national survey of the American prison system she describes 17.85 percent of them as custodial penitentiaries; 32.15 percent as custody oriented; 17.85 percent as mixed; 14.30 percent as treatment oriented; and 17.85 percent as treatment centers (Strickland, 1976, p. 206).

By 1971 there were 34 states that had completely separate facilities for women, and 2 federal institutions that housed women (Schweber, 1984). In 1992 there were 14 federal institutions that housed women (U.S. Federal Bureau of Prisons, 1992) with at least 1 state prison in every state, with the exception of New Hampshire and West Virginia, states that boarded out female inmates to neighboring state prisons or housed them in county jails.

The state prison system in the last four decades has not changed a great deal. Today they house primarily poor, miseducated black females, and are a major employer of white males. The 1990 American Correctional Association Directory reported that from 1985 to 1989, 43 states opened a total of 54 new adult correctional facilities, including 119 prisons, 12 camps, and 23 other facilities (e.g., health and reception centers). These new facilities represent 89,000 additional beds and cells. In 1994 Congress allocated $22 billion to the Federal Bureau of Prisons to build additional federal prison beds and funds for 100,000 new police officers. (See chapter 8 for a more detailed discussion.)

The Privatization of Prisons

Unfortunately, due to the reported overcrowding of America's prisons, correctional services have begun to reinstate a system that in the past had failed to protect the rights of its female inmates. That system, briefly discussed in the previous section, is the Dread-Lessee System. When the female prison population begun to increase in 1985, so did the privately managed prisons, jumping from 1,345 inmates to 49,154 inmates in 1994 with a projected 65,000 by the end of 1995 (*New York Times*, 8/95, p. 7). Our nation's response to the crises in drugs, unemployment, undereducation, mental illness, and the like is not to deal with those social ills but to find a way to control and capture those female prisoners who have no voice in where they live, sleep, or eat. The enticement for prison officials is the cost savings per female prisoner. In a recent study regarding cost savings by special Joint Committee Tennessee State Legislature it was reported "that the Corrections Corporation of America" prison cost an average of $35.18 per inmate per day, compared with an average of $35.76 in two state prisons. (*New York Times*, 8/19/95, p. 7). When you subtract $35.18 from $35.76 the cost savings is a modest 58 cents. However they report that they would save $150,000 a year, partly by hiring non-union guards and offering their guards stock options rather than a pension plan. Table 1.1 provides a comparison of state government–operated and private prison lessee corporation per diem costs.

Table 1.1 Comparison of State Government and Private Contractor Per Diem Costs Per Prisoner in Dollars

Private Facility	Government (estimated)	Contractor
St. Mary's, KY	28.00	26.89
Beattyville, KY	32.00	26.89
Owensboro, KY	N/A	27.50*
Grants, NM	80.00	69.75
Winnfield, LA	29.50	26.00*
Cleveland, TX	42.53	35.25

Private Facility	Government (estimated)	Contractor
Venus, TX	42.53	35.25
Kyle, TX	42.53	34.79
Bridgeport, TX	42.53	34.79

*Estimated Costs

Source: U.S. Government Accounting Office, GAO/GGD-91-21 Private Prisons, February 1991, p. 16.

This form of prison movement has been experimented with in other countries—Great Britain, Australia, and France—but the United States leads in this form of correction (Ethridge and Marquart, 1993). In the United States in 1991 there were 15 private prison lessee corporations that managed male, female, and juvenile inmates. Five of these prison lessee corporations were exclusively for female inmates and nine had a mixed population. Table 1.2 lists private corporations that imprison females.

Table 1.2 Private Corporations That Incarcerate Females

ST	Contractor	Location	Inmate Sex/ Capacity	Date Operational
CA	Eclectic Comm. Inc.	Live Oak	Female 200	Aug. 1988
CA	Wackenhut Correc. Corp.	McFarland	Male/Female* 200	Jan. 1989
CO	Wackenhut Correc. Corp.	Denver	Male/Female* 150	May 1987
FL	Correction Corp. of America	Brooksville	Male/Female* 252	Oct. 1988
FL	Wackenhut Correc. Corp.	Monroe County	Male/Female* 320	Feb. 1990
KY	Dismas Charities Inc.	Owensboro	Female 100	July 1990
MI	Wackenhut Correc. Corp.	Detroit	Male/Female* 400	April 1987
NM	Correction Corp. of America	Grants	Female 200	June 1989
NM	Correction Corp. of America	Santa Fe	Male/Female* 256	Aug. 1986
NY	Wackenhut Correc. Corp.	New York	Male/Female* Juvenile 100	Oct. 1989
TN	Correction Corp. of America	Chattanooga	Female 117	Oct. 1984

ST	Contractor	Location	Inmate Sex/ Capacity	Date Operational
TX	Concepts Inc.	Bridgeport	Female 100	N/A
TX	Wackenhut Correc. Corp	San Antonio Bexar County	Male/Female* 619	April 1988
WA	Esmor Inc.	Seattle	Male/Female* 68	July 1989

*Number of female inmates is not listed separately.
Source: U.S. General Accounting Office, GAO/GGD-91-21, *Private Prisons*, February 1991, pp. 33–44.

Private corporations primarily provide services for state correctional services. At the time of this writing the federal government does not contract with private prison firms, with the exception of Esmor Correctional Services, which operates a detention center for the Immigration and Naturalization Service (INS). However Esmor Correctional Services Corporation recently lost its contract following an uprising at Elizabeth, NJ, where an investigation by the INS "found that Esmor, in cutting costs, had failed to train guards and that they abused detainees by beating them or putting them in leg irons" (*New York Times*, 8/19/95, p. 7). The federal government has boarded prisoners in states that do operate private prisons and the Bureau of Prisons has announced that it will turn over operation of four newly built minimum and low security prisons to private companies. They do, however, board federal prisoners in states that do use private corporations. The first private and first women's facility opened in 1984 in Chattanooga, Tennessee. In 1987 Detroit, Michigan, opened the largest locally operated private facility (400 beds). This number of beds had increased to 14,000 by January 1989 (Johnson and Ross, 1990).

There are those who believe that the conservative movement of the 1980s and the election of Ronald Reagan as president—who advocated more private sector involvement—were the catalysts that revitalized a somewhat dying interest in private prisons. It was also President Reagan's administration that began to downsize government operations as an example of movement away from government control and support for further private sector involvement, even in jail and prison operations. In addition, the President's Commission on Privatization wrote that this "may well be seen by future historians as one of the most important developments in American political and economic life of the 20th century" (Ethridge & Marquart 1993, p. 30).

Even though there wasn't a directive or presidential order (that I am aware of) specifically for prison officials, the entrepreneurs who have always provided some limited services for prisons (medical, educational and food services), like any business entity, seized the opportunity to make money. Prison officials who are overburdened with crowding issues and escalating prison costs welcomed the chance to shake themselves loose from an enormous system that needed major costly attention. Also, there are already numerous private sector contracts that involve prisoners, such as halfway houses or prisoner's community reentry programs. With private contractors looking for economic opportunities, the public sector appears to be the most eager to expand.

History of the Texas Prison Lessee System: Women, Slaves, and Other Victims

As previously mentioned in this chapter, prisoners during the colonial era were required to pay for their room and board. Following the Civil War there was a lack of free slave labor and an increasing prison population that became overwhelming for the authorities. Many of those who were filling the jail cells were slaves. A combination of these two factors—need for labor and free slaves—provided the climate for the establishment of a slave lessee system. In general, punishment in Texas—prior to the institution of prisons—consisted of capital burning, boiling, beheading, hanging, splitting the tongue for slander, branding for the thief, and castration for the rapist (Crown, 1964, p. 17). Most of these punishments were directed toward white prisoners; punishments for black slaves came much later.

The Texas penitentiary system got underway in 1839. Punishments varied, but capital punishment was instituted for four types of crimes. Among them was "advising or conspiring with a slave to rebel or cause an insurrection." Kidnapping a slave carried a penalty of hard labor from 3 to 15 years, while aiding a slave to escape brought imprisonment for 3–5 years (Crown, p. 33).

Elizabeth Hofman was the first woman admitted to prison in 1854; a servant girl convicted of infanticide was sentenced to a one-year term; and "by 1865, ten Negro women were inmates, working as cooks in the penitentiary kitchen, but the necessity of supplementing their labor with male convicts proved morally unsatisfactory" (Crown, p. 85). Therefore, prison officials decided to assign the women prisoners to private homes as servants for a mere $1 per month labor fee.

By 1871 the Texas state government was advertising for bidders for the leasing of the penitentiary system. This was prompted by the apparent debt Texas had incurred in generating the system. Texas's experiences in lessee systems was guided by the Penitentiary Act, which gave prison officials the authority to locate a cotton mill within the prison. Female prisoners along with men worked in these factories and slept in adjunct cells. These sleeping arrangements were in direct violation of laws that required the separation of the sexes.

With little regard for their welfare, black slaves were leased out to work as farm laborers and house servants. Due to the lack of immigrants who located in Texas, the lessee system flourished in the South. By 1880 all 11 confederate states had some form of leasing inmate labor system. With this new penal system more and more prisoners were coming into the system. By 1866 Texas leased its prisoners to two railroad companies. Numerous complaints of inmate abuse began to be made public. For example, "a Negro convict on the Patton plantation in Brazoria County had received 604 lashes by actual count on his naked back shortly before a prison visit of concerned citizens" (Crown, p. 103).

Like other Southern states, Texas found itself with large numbers of slaves following the Civil War, many of whom were now entering these prisons. Prior to the Civil War slaves were not subjected to imprisonment. The white master was judge and jury and inflicted whatever punishment he deemed necessary. Slaves who were found guilty of murder, arson, or insurrection were hanged (Crown, p. 86). Following the Civil War, uneducated slaves were now liable for their own crimes, so the state prison facilities began to overflow. In 1865 negroes or slaves accounted for 40 percent of the Texas prison population.

The railroad leasing system was eventually phased out amidst the abuse of prisoners and replaced in 1871 with private companies taking over full control of prison property, a system that lasted 15 years. The state of Texas turned a profit and thought they had solved the prison problem. However, they were still plagued by the mistreatment of prisoners by guards and the lack of medical attention. With a legislative inquiry that found lessees' treatment abusive, the system was abolished in 1883. But the state authorities felt they had benefited from the leasing system and so continued a somewhat modified system, in spite of the legislative vote to abolish it. So from 1883 to 1912 the state continued to lease out prisoners to local companies. For instance, in 1907 the female population was incarcerated on Johnson Farms, while men were scattered in labor camps. Of these, 130—"the majority being

Negroes were convicted chiefly of theft and burglary. The ten or twelve white women had been sentenced for murder" (Crown, p. 197). When charges arose regarding male employees and female inmates (most of whom were black), these women were transferred from the lessee system to another location such as "agricultural and factory labors" (p. 198). In 1912 the contract lessee system ceased to exist in Texas. However, decades later Texas is still one of the nation's leaders with more than 30 privately operated prisons (*New York Times*, 8/19/95, p. 7).

Again, Texas was faced with a growing prison population increasing from 112.8 percent between 1980 and 1986, from 26,576 in 1980 to 40,227 (Crown, p. 35), most of whom are African American and other minorities (Native and Mexican American). Texas was also faced with a tight state economy and no money for new prison construction. As in the 1800s, the politicians looked for a way out. In January 1987 several bills were introduced that would once again allow the state to lease out its female prison population. Unlike the 1800s, Texas did attempt to place some strict legislative control on private prison vendors. As such they were required to comply with federal court orders and accreditation requirements; agree that a maximum of 2,000 medium or minimum security inmates were to be housed in units holding no more than 500 inmates; offer services equal to the states; agree to a contract length not to exceed three years; agree that the vendor had no authority to grant parole dates or set release; give good conduct award time; allow the furlough and transfer of classified inmates; and agree that inmates were to remain in the legal custody of the State Department of Correction (p. 38). A 1987 request for proposals resulted in two prison corporations being selected, Becon-Wackenhut, a partnership of Becon Correction Company and Wackenhut Services, and Correction Corporation of America, who operate private services for the state.

The Correction Corporation of America operates a number of private prisons for women in many locations throughout the United States (see Table 1.2). Prison staff, however, monitor the operation of the private contractors for compliance with required regulations. Their findings criticized both companies for the following: inadequate health services; insufficient programs to keep prisoners occupied; attributing abusive treatment of inmates to the inexperience of guards; filling staff positions slowly or not at all; the lack of educational programs for Spanish-speaking persons; minimal inmate population in substance abuse programs; and the absence of self-monitoring (Crown, p. 42). The prison corporation felt that the audit was unfair since it was conducted during a shakedown, and the corporation was awarded the contract for another two years. When one of the corporations that incarcerates Texas women prisoners—Correction Corporation of America—was battling a lawsuit involving a claim of wrongful death of an inmate, the corporation did not inform its shareholders in its annual report of the $100 million litigation case (Johnson and Ross, 1990, p. 355).

Many ethical and legal liability issues emerge when private prison staff use deadly force. Following the caning of an American student in Singapore, six state legislatures, with Mississippi leading the charge, are debating whether or not to whip prisoners. Who is ultimately responsible (having the legal authority) for the welfare of the prisoners: the vendor or the state? The fixing of legal responsibility is required in terms of where or who will pay the lawsuit. This question and many others must be addressed prior to the placement of female prisoners in the care of others. With the increasing prison population reaching its all-time high in 1988—from 304,692 in 1980 to 604,824 in 1988—it is important that these issues be addressed and resolved.

It is disturbing to realize that private prison managers spend a great deal of money on lobbying and other marketing strategies. For example, Correction Corporation of America spent over $1.5 million in these areas during the period 1985–87, a substantial amount for a company that managed only 1,715 beds at nine facilities during this same period (Johnson and Ross, 1990, p. 353). Nevertheless, as a consequence of these efforts, they now manage many facilities that house women (see Table 1.2).

It is difficult to give a clear picture at this time of the potential growth in private prisons. However, if the private corporations continue to lobby, spend large sums of money on marketing strategies, cut cost-per-prisoner care, and build prisons with less red tape than traditional prisons, construction companies will in fact entice lawmakers and state officials to explore the options for future expansion. The economics of privatization must be closely studied. For in times of high unemployment, where the government has taken a lead in providing job opportunities, such employment would be seriously hampered by private intervention into correctional services. The negative impact privatization would have on the economy would also be felt by the downsizing of civil services, due to the fact that private industry does not operate in a structured civil services system. In addition, "loss of important training opportunities ... provided by agreement ... could be devastating not just for the minorities and women, but also for the private sector, which depends upon government to provide an adequately trained labor force" (Johnson and Ross, p. 353). Government could intervene and monitor hiring and set contract quotas. This would have to be paid for with public money and therefore, would not be cost effective in meeting the cost-containment strategies set by corrections.

While there may be some advantages in moving toward privatization of prisons, these appear to be mainly benefiting the state or federal government or the private vendors. Who speaks for the prisoner? What advantages do they gain from this system? An example of how corrections have attempted to help the inmate was tried in California. About 200 inmates were contracted out to process meat, fish, and poultry for a state-run institution. They were paid 20–80 cents an hour with one day off their sentence for every day worked. They would learn a skill and have a few dollars when released. The state had paid $14 million a year for the same work, and it was assumed that this new approach would benefit the prisoner and the state. Even though these kinds of prisons can benefit both inmates and the prison administration, their expansion is very slow. In raising the above concerns, there are others that should always be considered by states, including Texas, prior to a written contract agreement. They are as follows:

1. Prison officials should do a thorough background check of private vendors;

2. A strict and very detailed evaluation system should be established before the contract is signed;

3. A very specific in-depth cost-savings analysis should be undertaken;

4. Determine where there is potential/ongoing support for the venture;

5. All rules must be clarified; and

6. Prison officials should be barred from purchasing stock in private prison corporations.

We must also remember that, historically, nonprofit organizations are usually more concerned about humanistic issues; whereas for-profit corporations are concerned with, and place emphasis on, making money. Therefore, contractors must be scrutinized and held accountable for the lives of prisoners entrusted to their care. Without a firm commitment from private entrepreneurs, who are more often than not driven by profit motives and emphasize cash flow above and beyond human needs, the prison population will surely suffer.

Other Experiences with Private Prisons

Between 1850 and 1950, California, Louisiana, Michigan, Oklahoma, and Texas had privately operated prisons, but these were phased
out amid charges of inmate abuse (U.S. General Accouting Office,
GAO/GGD-91-21, February 1991, p. 2). These same states, with the
exception of Oklahoma and Louisiana, have reinstituted the lessee system that once had failed them.

As of January 1990 there were 41 states and the District of Columbia that were under court order to reduce their overcrowded facilities
(U.S. General Accouting Office, February, 1991, pp. 8–9). The quick
fix now is to lease these prisoners to those who can build facilities much
quicker and with less bureaucratic red tape. The 1991 GAO/GDD, report
stated that in New Mexico it took nine months for a contracted lessee
program to build a facility for its women inmates where it would have
taken three years for the state government to do so. There are apparently standards that state governments must adhere to, from which
private corporations are exempt. This would make you wonder if the
private prison facilities are at least adhering to minimum standards for
the safety and welfare of the prisoners. In addition, if the private corporations move so quickly, how do they protect their investments? Do
they lobby for longer sentences or fail to implement education or work
programs designed to reduce recidivism? Corporate intrusion into
human services areas is serious business.

Federal Prison Development
and the African American Female

The U.S. federal prison system for women is one that grew out of
the vigorous efforts of female organizations to sensitize the public to
the need to develop a separate system for women. During the nineteenth century there were no federal prison facilities to house women.
If there was a need to house women who committed federal offenses,
they were boarded in state correctional facilities. As previously mentioned, most state prisons practiced racial segregation, in which the federal government willingly participated by housing women in a racist
and segregated system. For example, a large number of black women
convicted under the Volstead Act (1919) and the Harrison Act (1914),
and infected with "loathsome diseases" (a euphemism for veneral disease) were housed in state reformatories in Rhode Island, where prison

authorities used these physical problems to justify segregation of the races into separate wings or single rooms (Rafter, 1985, p. 153).

It was not until the end of the Civil War that the federal female inmate population began to grow. When its population reached 15,000 in 1890 (Browker, 1978, p. 149), and after the efforts of women groups, the first federal facility was built on 500 acres of rural farmland in Alderson, West Virginia. Opened in 1927, it housed 50 women in each of its 14 cottages. By 1929 there were over 250 inmates. This federal facility housed "women from rural south and northeast cities, white, colored, Indian, Mexican, Chinese and Japanese women" (Lekkerk-erker, 1931, p. 205), sentenced to serve one year or more prison terms. Approximately 66 percent of these women had committed violations of the drug laws. Recognizing the reason for their commitment, the facilities developed drug treatment programs that centered on social and psychological factors associated with drug dependency. In an attempt to break the drug habits of the inmates, the programs focused on not only the medical aspects of treatment but also incorporated out-door activities, occupational therapy, and intensive, specialized educa-tional and prolonged aftercare. Other programs offered to the female inmate population were the stereotypical female occupations such as homemaking, stenography, typing, business, English, general science, farming, mechanical knitting, dairying, and power sewing.

During the 1920s Congress passed several laws against organized crime and prohibition, which resulted in steep increases in the entire federal prison population. To manage this increase, in 1930 federal leg-islation created the Bureau of Prisons (BOP) and authorized the con-struction of additional federal correctional facilities. Following the con-struction of these facilities from 1940 to 1980, the prison population began to stabilize around 20,000–25,000. However, since the 1980s the inmate population, augmented by the war on drugs and illegal aliens, has soared to over 50,000. Between 1985 and 1989 the federal government responded to this dramatic increase by adding an addi-tional four prisons at a cost of $183 million, adding another 2,600 beds to its federal prison system (U.S. General Accounting Office, October 1991, p. 150). As previously mentioned, in 1993 Congress allocated $22 billion to build federal prison cells.

In conclusion, the U.S. criminal justice system was designed dur-ing the colonial era to house those so-called fallen women who were primarily white and of the servant class. With the import of African slaves in 1619 these newcomers were also indentured servants until the

1660s, when legal enslavement of blacks for a lifetime was instituted. For over 40 years whites and Africans were indentured servants, until it was recognized by the founding fathers that America's economy depended largely on keeping the African slaves enslaved. From that day on economic factors influenced the development of plantation prison farms—the prison farms of the South—which doomed black women to a life of servitude without release. Black American females were not confined to these early colony jails because it was not profitable, so they were punished and then returned to the plantation master.

As the nation moved into the era of emancipation, the judicial system began to weave a web of Jim Crow laws. These laws were created to be broken by uneducated and docile African slaves, whose once free skills or labor were needed to rebuild the fallen South and to keep the economy moving forward. In order to harness this no longer free source of labor, Jim Crowism would lead the freed slave to jails and plantation lessee farms where they would be brutalized and literally worked to death. Texas was one of the Southern states that capitalized on the lessee system. Because of its location, Texas lacked the large European immigrant population to fill its needs. It did, however, have a very large, uneducated, and hungry freed slave population. Like other states, Texas laws funneled thousands of slaves into their prisons (legalized slavery) and then leased out their services. As America became more civilized, this form of lessee was abolished and replaced with the more civilized British penal system. Then as the country struggled with the various forms of incarceration models, the segregation of black women—who were now overrepresented in the custodial setting—continued to exist until the early 1900s. Even after it was recognized that women needed separate facilities, black females continued to be segregated in separate cottages and forced to work at the worst jobs, while their white counterparts were assigned to more pleasant jobs or sent to school. The federal prison system also developed separate facilities for women when certain laws were passed (for example, the Harrison Act) that brought large numbers of black women into the federal prison system. The U.S. prison system of the twentieth century continues to grow with the incarceration of the descendants of the African slaves, who were brought to this country to help secure an economic base for white America. These same descendants are now supporting the U.S. economic base in a different manner: their incarceration provides jobs for primarily white U.S. males who are employed in record numbers at all levels of the criminal justice system.

Chapter 2

Criminology and
the African American Female

*Theoretical Perspective of Female Criminality
with Emphasis on the African-American Female*

Criminologists, sociologists, biologists, and other investigators have all attempted to discover the reasons for the female criminal. Within these various disciplines there have been numerous studies that delve into the nature and cause of male criminality. However, the same level of attention and research has not been equally shared with female offenders in general and more specifically African American female offenders. This may be attributed to the following reasons: the lack of opportunities for African Americans to conduct research in the field of criminology (discussed in the next section); a field that is dominated by white male researchers; and the fact that this area is a politically sensitive issue that, if fully understood, could cause considerable concern and mean committing a substantial amount of resources to change or eliminate an unfair social structure. This social structure has facilitated behavior that has often resulted in the overrepresentation of African Americans being incarcerated.

Black Criminologists

According to Katheryn Russell (1992) there are fewer than 50 blacks in the nation who have received doctorates in Criminology or Criminal Justice (p. 675). In addition, between 1980 and 1990 there were 399 Americans awarded doctorates in criminology, with only 27 (8 percent) being awarded to blacks. Of these 27, 15 were awarded to African American women (p. 876). With the dearth of black criminologists in the field, and the need to address—empirically and in depth—why there is an overrepresentation of African American women in prison and the increase of black-on-black crimes, there is a real need to encourage African Americans to study criminology. Such researchers would be more culturally sensitized to issues that affect the black community as a whole.

A black criminologist who has an Afro-centric understanding of how a specific research design might better address a minority community problem could uncover variable(s) overlooked in other research designs. Furthermore, without question, a black criminologist is likely to be more familiar than a white criminologist with "black life" and the black community (p. 677). The ever increasing number of African American women entering the criminal justice system and the total disregard—from an empirical standpoint—of the need to address their specific issues are other examples of social neglect and abuse. Minority women criminologists (the few that we have) must take charge and be allowed to provide their own account of themselves. Without their valuable input, white male criminologists will continue to focus on issues that they feel are important.

In the development of this chapter it was extremely difficult to sort out the appropriate early theories that may have relevance to African American female criminality. As a consequence, there is considerable question as to whether the theoretical assumptions from these early studies—that lack a significant number of African American female subjects or fail to note the subjects race/ethnicity—can logically be generalized to the criminality of African American females.

This chapter, however, will present those early studies for the historical information needed to adequately understand how certain ideologies and assumptions regarding African American female criminality have developed in the field of female criminality. Also, because of past fragmented and current speculative research that often contains major gaps in methodology (for example, failing to note research subjects' race), only those theories that have relevance to understanding African American female criminal behavior are emphasized and presented.

Biological and Sociological Theorists' Perspective on Female Criminology

One of the first major attempts to explain female criminality from a biological perspective was made in 1894 by Cesare Lombroso, an Italian psychiatrist. Lombroso and his son-in-law, William Ferrero, examined the skeletal remains of female inmates to see if there were signs of biological atavism or survival of primitive traits and characteristics, "particularly those of the females of nonwhite races" (Adler and Simon, 1979, p. 62). In other words, are certain physical traits in the female criminal absent from the normal, noncriminal female? His investigation resulted in the categorizing of the body part (skull and jawbone) to coincide with criminal behavior. For example, a prostitute had a heavy lower jaw and deep frontal sinuses, whereas a so-called fallen woman had a narrower forehead and prominent cheekbones (Lombroso and Ferrero, 1920, p. 29). Lombroso's study was severely criticized because of methodological inadequacies. First, his sample size was very small—47 prostitutes and 72 criminals—to which he later added other subjects to bring his numbers closer to 1,000. Second, his sample came from different geographic areas; and third, Lombroso's study lacked a standardized measurement by which to judge any anomalies.

Lombroso theorized that individuals developed differently within racial and sexual hierarchical lines, with white males at the top of the pyramids and females and nonwhite races at the bottom (Adler and Simon, 1979, p. 62). Apparently, when Lombroso mentioned race in his research his subjects were of the following ethnic groups: "Sicilian, Neapolitans, natives of March and Umbria, Venetians, Lombards, natives of Emilia, Tuscans, Ligurians, and Piedmontese" (Lombroso and Ferrero, 1915, p. 3). This early study set the tone in research literature, resulting in numerous studies that sought to explain female criminality through biological explanations. For example, in its twenty-first–century study the Neuropsychiatric Institute of the University of California at Los Angeles has explored whether females commit acts of violence during premenstrual periods (PMS crimes); and Cowie, Cowie, and Slater have identified large size in females, as a possible cause for aggressive behavior (Crites, 1978, p. 28).

Like Lombroso, Sigmund Freud also felt that women were biologically deficient. Freud contended that women were envious of male masculinity and therefore, because of some anatomical differences, would turn to antisocial or deviant behavior. According to Freud it was the lack of a penis that made women envious; that women are traumatized by the lack of a penis; and this envy translated into vengeful behavior. As such, "Women become mothers trying to replace the lost penis with a baby" (Crites, 1978, p. 16). Following Freud and Lombroso, there were and still are those who imply contradictory notions of female criminality. One of those theorists was sociologist William Isaac Thomas. In his book *Sex and Society* (1907) he severely criticized anthropologists for their notion that women committed crimes because they had anatomical deficiencies, like a small or inferior brain. Yet he built his thinking around the biological work of Lombroso by emphasizing the physical differences among the races. He stated the following:

> What we look for most in the female is femininity, and when we find the opposite in her, we must conclude as a rule that there must be some anomaly.... In the portraits of Red Indian and Negro beauties, whom it is difficult to recognize for women, so huge are their jaws and cheekbones, so hard and coarse their features, and the same is often in the case of their crania and brain [p. 112].

It was Thomas's contention that "A woman entered prostitution to satisfy a desire for excitement and response; as a woman prostitution, in one form or another, was a most likely avenue to satisfy those needs" (Pollock, 1978, p. 45). In addition to the racist notions of Thomas, other researchers of this era focused on women's sexual behavior as the cause of female criminality.

Eleanore and Sheldon Glueck's research also focused on whether or not biological factors determined if a female would turn to a life of crime: "The Gluecks, as did the earlier researchers, identified both social and heredity factors" that they felt would contribute to the likelihood of criminal behavior (Pollock, 1978, p. 16). As in most investigative studies of this era, the sexual habits of the incarcerated female were always examined. "This may have been necessary for the large number of incarcerated prostitutes; however, in the case of other crimes the sexual life of the offender was important only because she was female" (Flowers, 1987, p. 96).

In their 1934 study of physical and psychological traits of 500 hundred delinquent girls, the Gluecks concluded the following: "Female criminality results in large part from biological and economic factors.

Furthermore, they found that an extremely high percentage of delinquent girls came from abnormally large families, were mentally defective, and had been arrested mainly for illicit sexual behavior, and that criminality was likely to be intergenerational" (Flowers, 1987, p. 9).

Apparently, the Gluecks began their investigation by looking for the answer to criminal behavior but, unfortunately, became advocates for long prison terms and sterilization of those women judged to be "defective delinquents." Fortunately, this biased thinking did not receive rave reviews from the public.

Otto Pollak, another sociologist, reviewed in a 1950 study data of U.S., British, French, and German researchers in an effort to draw some conclusions as to why there were so many conflicting theories in female criminology. Pollak, who apparently was also influenced by Lombroso and Freud, felt that female criminal behavior was sexually motivated, while males were economically motivated. He, like the previously mentioned investigators who focused much of their attention on the sexual behavior of females, subscribed to the notion that women could easily hide their crimes by faking orgasms and concealing menstruation. By hiding these two natural female processes, Pollak felt that women were deceitful, and therefore some of their crimes would be hidden and go unnoticed. Pollak was one of the first early investigators who believed that females received preferential treatment in the criminal justice system, an assumption that might have been true for the white female prison population but certainly not for the black female population. This will be further explored in the statistical presentation in chapter 3.

Frances Kellor and Jean Weidensall also conducted significant research in the 1800s and early 1900s. Kellor—like Freud, Thomas, and Lombroso—compared physical qualities of female prisoners to those of the so-called normal female. In her research she discredited Lombroso's finding because his study could not be replicated (Pollock-Byrne, 1990, p. 13). Kellor believed as follows:

> The women's life experiences and generally deprived backgrounds had much to do with their entry into criminality. For instance, ... many women criminals came from the ranks of domestic services ... proportionally, many women were employed in domestic services; inadequate salaries spurred women to steal; workers engaged in domestic services were typically unskilled and unable to do anything else; domestic service was an easy route to prostitution; and employment bureaus were often procurement places for prostitution [Pollock-Byrne, 1990, p. 13].

Kellor, who received a law degree from Cornell University in 1897, was one of the earliest researchers who, through her feminist concerns, advocated the recognition of the rights of Negro women and openly attacked Lombroso's biological interpretation of crime (Freedman, 1981, p. 112).

In addition, Jean Weidensall conducted research on the grounds of New York State's largest women's prison: Bedford Hills. Weidensall also measured female prisoners' physical characteristics: height, weight, hand grip, and visual acuity. She further compared schoolgirls and working women to the mental characteristics of reformatory prisoners. Weidensall was skeptical of the prisoners' low IQ because the normal IQ test scores had been based on those of college students. The results of her research found that reformatory prisoners were dull, of lower intelligence, unthinking, unstable, and easily frustrated. Based on her research, Weidensall believed that there were three types of female prisoners: intelligent but lazy, real criminals, and those who were unintelligent and easily led into a life of crime (Pollock-Byrne, 1990).

Vedder and Sommerville's study of incarcerated delinquent girls focused attention on the importance of family pathologies. They contended that "special attention should be given to girls, taking into consideration their constitutional, biological, psychological differences" (Vedder and Sommerville, 1970, p. 153). However, they failed to tell us what these differences were. Ironically, Vedder and Sommerville's investigations do note the large number of black incarcerated women (a factor apparently unnoticed by prison administrations then and now) in their sample and make the following racist statement to justify their presence:

> The conflict and frustrations of the normal adolescent are compounded ... for the delinquent Negro girls.... The black girl is, in fact, the antithesis of American beauty. However loved she may be by her mother, family and community, she has no real basis of feminine attractiveness on which to build a sound feminine narcissism. When to her physical unattractiveness is added a discouraging, depreciating mother-family community environment, there is a damaged self-concept and an impairment of her feminine narcissism which will have profound consequence for her character development [1970, p. 159].

The above statement completely ignores the economic, racist, and sexist factors that black women must endure and reduces their criminality to a state of femininity seen through the biased eyes of American white women.

These early theories all tend to view female criminality as sexually motivated and rooted in some biological or psychological deficiency. As we entered the turbulent times of the 1960s there were those who began to refute biological and psychological theories of female criminality and replaced them with different perspectives: that other factors like racism, women's sex role, economics, and poverty might have had a bearing on female criminal behavior (Arnold, 1995; Simon, 1975; Weiss, 1976). It was also during this time that we began to see additional studies that cited the significant number of African American women in the prison populations. This recognition might have been sparked by the 1960 civil rights movement that sought justice for millions of disenfranchised Americans who were in different social positions (for example, the elderly, mentally ill, handicapped, minorities, and women). Certainly since the civil rights movement white women have benefited significantly, outnumbering black women in all economic and educational advances.

As previously stated, research dealing specifically with African American women prisoners has been virtually absent in the literature. In the discussion that follows the most relevant studies are presented, selected for their attempts to identify a theoretical basis for African American female criminality.

No other era in the history of the United States saw as many changes affecting women as those that emerge from the civil rights movement. The one that is found most often cited in the literature as a theoretical basis for the increase in female criminal behavior is the women's liberation movement.

In an effort to determine the effect that women's liberation movement had on female criminal behavior, Lawrence French (Winter, 1978) analyzed the arrest records of the North Carolina prison population. This investigation was in response to the statistical data that showed the number of female offenders increased by 108 percent between 1960 and 1974. French's analysis revealed that over half the male prisoners were black and over 66 percent of the females were black. The black females in the study were classified as having lower occupational levels, with 82 percent not completing high school. It is suspected, at least for the North Carolina prison population, that other forces, such as sexism and racism, not just the women's movement, were the cause of this large African American female North Carolina prison population. For within the Southern states there has continued to be an endemic prejudice against African Americans in general.

In another similar study by Joan Mandle (1981) urban arrest data were cited for 1962–1975 and then analyzed to see if the women's liberation movement had an impact on the increase in crimes. Mandle's findings revealed the following: "urban arrest rates for women have risen in every category of crime in the violent crime index and in the property crime index; however, the arrest rate for men has increased accordingly for all but larceny, where in 1962 women were responsible for 19 percent of the larcenies and 38 percent in 1975" (p. 11).

Apparently, this increase in the rate of imprisonment of males as well as the females cannot be attributed solely to the women's movement. There were other factors that impacted on the crime rate (for example, poverty) that in turn affected arrest numbers. There will be a discussion regarding the implications of poverty on crime rate below.

Two women sociologists, Freda Adler and Rita Simon (1979), also attempted to join the ranks of those who wanted to explain female criminality by the impact of the women's liberation movement. Adler believed that as women gained more freedom from their household tasks, through economic opportunity, work place equality, and the women's liberation movement they would become involved in a life of crime because of these new exposures to freedom and wealth. She further believed that as women left their homes to compete for jobs in the old boy arena, women would become more like men, and therefore more vulnerable to criminal elements. One of her arguments to substantiate this notion was that black women in the United States had been liberated far longer than white women, which has proven to be detrimental and resulted in their overrepresentation in the prison population. Adler states that "one can appreciate where white women are headed as liberated criminals in coming years" (1975, p. 154). In other words once white women are liberated they will, like black women, end up behind prison bars. Adler, a female and a sociologist, completely misinterprets the status of the black woman's position in U.S. society—jinxed—first because they are women and secondly because they happen to be black: the double whammy.

Simon also wrote that "as women's opportunities to commit crimes increase, so will their deviant behavior, and the types of crimes they commit will much more closely resemble crimes committed by men" (1975, p. 48). These two women's theories of female criminality are so simplistic because they completely ignore the complex social system where poverty, racism, and poor education run rampant in urban America.

Clarice Feinman (1984) in her defense of black women states the following: "In claiming that black women are more criminal than white because they have been liberated longer distorts history. Black women had to leave their homes to work and are often heads of households because of poverty and racial discrimination and not because they chose to do so" (p. 20).

In an important article by Gary Hill and Elizabeth Crawford (1990), Adler and Simon's theories are further shown to be not representative of black female criminality. In their research they explored "the relative effectiveness of traditional criminologist theories in accounting for the involvement of white and black women, respectively, in crime" (p. 61). The subjects in their research were from a sample of 922 black and 878 white females between the ages of 18 and 23 who responded to a survey by the National Opinion Research Center. In order to determine the correct variables to be studied, the researchers reviewed theoretical literature and from that review decided upon seven broad theory headings to explain crimes committed: social control, liberation/gender role socialization, self-esteem, deprivation, strain, urbanism, and maturation. The following discussion of these variables will help to clarify why it is so important to include social factors in the study of criminality.

Social Control Theory lost popularity in the 1960s, but it has recently reemerged. This theory is primarily grounded in the notion that bonding in certain social groups like family and church are a necessary entity in a healthy life style. It is the lack of these natural ties that can increase the possibility of committing crimes. Variables selected by Hill and Crawford from social control theory were family, church, and community.

Liberation/Gender Socialization Theory develops the notion that women are socialized differently from men (for example, female passiveness). The variable selected for study was sex role.

Self/Concept Theory looks at how one views oneself. It is evaluative in nature and in the study includes a set of ten questions to uncover the level of one's self esteem.

Deprivation Theory posits that low socioeconomic status and the deprivation associated with this status would closely correlate criminal behavior. Total family income and highest grade completed were selected to measure this theory's ability to predict behavior.

Strain Theory can be characterized as the frustrations of society's many constraints to an individual gaining access to opportunities that are afforded others. The variables measured here were occupational aspiration, unemployment rate, and the gap between educational aspirations and educational expectations.

Urbanism Theory, as it relates to criminal behavior, suggests that the urban environment lends itself to providing the social control and opportunities to learn how to commit crimes. The variables measured here were respondent residence.

Maturation Theory suggests that because younger persons commit more crimes than older persons, psychological development may play an important role in whether or not the person will commit a crime. The age of the respondent was the final variable selected.

These selected independent and theory driven variables were then analyzed in relationship to dependent variables: crime, drugs, major and minor property offenses, assault, and hustling. Again, Hill and Crawford explored these theories in their attempt to account for black and white female criminality in a comparative manner. Because this chapter deals with the theoretical perspectives of black women criminality, only those significant results reported by Hill and Crawford regarding this population will be emphasized. Results regarding white female criminality will only be presented when needed to clarify results or for comparison. In their analyses Hill and Crawford found the following:

> First, education, which was significant for whites but in a direction opposite to prediction, works as expected for blacks, that is, educational achievement decreases the odds of involvement in both major or minor property offenses. Second, gaps between educational aspirations and achievement is positively related to overall crime. Finally, proximity to the central city of a standard metropolitan statistical area (SMSA)* positively influenced the probability of illegal crime [p. 615].

Stated in simple terms, uneducated black women who live in large urban cities are more likely to be involved in crime. Hill and Crawford were unable to fully test the prediction of the seven theories with the data analyzed. However, they did offer some interesting commentary on the criminality of the black female and prevailing theory predictability.

First, the study noted that the independent variables were more useful in understanding the rate of crime among white than black women. This factor suggests that "the empirical neglect of the black

---

Populations set by the federal government.

female offender has had important consequences for the development of theory" (p. 621). Second, the overall effect of the application of the model's theoretical construct to predict the black female crime rate was not as strong. However, there was a "clustering of effect for whites within the social-psychological measures, in comparison with that for blacks within the blocks of structural/deprivation variable, which suggests that the unique position of black women in the structure of power relations in society has profound effects not shared by their white counterparts" (p. 621). In other words, black women on one hand are liberated because they must earn a living for their family—often because society has limited opportunities for their mates—resulting in her assuming the breadwinner role in the family. This research is one of the few studies that acknowledges that black females may experience things differently from their white counterparts.

As we continue to look for a theory for black female criminality, the complexity of establishing a concrete set of predictable variables that can adequately explain this situation was presented in a compilation of studies by Diane Lewis (1981). In her summary Lewis posits that there could be multiple factors and interrelationships of these factors that may account for black female criminality.

These interrelationships were presented in Lewis's article "Black Women Offenders and Criminal Justice—Some Theoretical Considerations." In examination of the literature, Lewis selected the most salient themes that appear to have a relationship to black female criminality for presentation in her article. They are as follows:

1. Age and other demographic characteristics;
2. Economics deprivation;
3. Status equality between sexes;
4. Distinctive socialization patterns;
5. Racism; and
6. Sexism.

As Lewis presents her review she notes that one of the first comprehensive studies to include the impact of demographic characteristics on black women was by Hans Von Hentig (1942). It was the first study of black women, ages 15 to 39, females he considered to be crime prone (pp. 238–39). In a very simplistic manner Von Hentig reviewed the arrest records of urban black and white women in these age groups and found that blacks made up the largest group of those arrested.

Lewis, however, states that the "black population nationally is younger than white" (p. 95), which may account for the increased number of black women arrested. In addition, Von Hentig points out that

> age appears a highly problematic variable when examining racial differences in arrest and incarceration rates. For example, black females composed only 18.9 percent of women age 18 to 24 in San Francisco, while white females were 52.4 percent of that age/sex group. Even though black women were less than 20 percent of all women, theoretically they were highly vulnerable to crime by virtue of their age, they composed 47 percent of those in the city actually sentenced in a six-month 1978 study [p. 95].

Lewis, like the writer of this book, believes that something other than age must be considered as a factor accounting for the overrepresentation of black women in the criminal justice system.

There have been numerous studies that recognize that black women come into the criminal justice system from an impoverished background (Adler, 1975; Wyrich, Owens, and Holloway, 1977; Becnel, 1978; Glick and Neto, 1977; Inglehart, 1981; Vega, Silverman, and Accardi, 1977; French, March 1978; Lewis and Bresler, 1981). In Lewis' 1981 study she again present data as follows: "34.4 percent of all black women 14 years and older were below the poverty level in 1980, compared to 14.3 percent of all white women" (p. 96). They preface their statement by reiterating that poverty alone cannot be totally blamed for the increase in the number of black women in prison, since there are more white women living in poverty. This writer agrees that there would be more white women living in poverty if the data are not weighted to account for the difference in the white and black populations. However, the 1983 poverty rate for white and black women as heads of households was 27 and 52 percent, respectively (Di Nitto and Dye, 1987, p. 53). When compared to "the rate of imprisonment of black women, at the end of 1982 it was 63 percent per 100,000 population, compared to 9 percent 100,000 for white women" (Flowers, 1987, p. 150), it is obvious that poverty must be seriously considered. There hasn't been much change, as reported by the 1990 U.S. census population data, that sets the percentage of single head of household families below poverty level at 23.2 percent for whites and 44.5 percent for blacks.

In reflecting status equality, there are those who believe that men commit more crimes than women because their position in society requires them to provide for their families, which may predispose them to commit crimes at a greater rate (Scutt, 1975). Then there are those who believe that the high crime rate among black women is due to their perceived status equality in the workplace, which has afforded these women the opportunities to commit crimes. Still there are others who contend that when white women gain their workplace equality status with their white male counterparts these women too will commit as many crimes. Lewis points out that white male-female sex ratio and black male-female sex ratio are very different. In addition, the earnings of black males and females are much closer than for white males and females. This may in part be due to the fact that black men die at an earlier age than black women, thus black women outnumber black men in the workplace and as head of households. Jocelynne Scutt (1978) states that the increased crime rate among black women could also be due to the fact that "black women are more often responsible for their families in much the same way the white male is responsible for his family" (p. 42).

Along with this responsibility comes the burden of supporting all aspects of the family circle. The African American female has reached this position through a socialization process that makes her the dominant figure in her family circle. White America has perpetuated this position of black woman as the central family figure by hiring her before her husband, brother, uncle, and her son. Freda Adler (1975) has hypothesized that the impact of slavery on the black family has caused the black female to become the dominant family figure. In this regard the black family structure was always a target of slave masters; the separation of family members, by selling off the strong males to the highest bidder, left the black female with the early burden of family management. Thus the foundation was laid and the black female was propelled into the forefront and continues to be kept there by social and structural boundaries placed upon her and her family by white America. Some view this position as breadwinner of the family as providing her with the opportunity to commit crime much like the white male, whose crime rate closely mirrors the black female offender. Consequently, through black female child-rearing practices these dominant characteristics are passed on from generation to generation and facilitated by society structural boundaries.

Lewis (1981) also addresses the issue of how children are socialized by comparing black and white children in her following statement:

> White children appear to be socialized to a higher differentiated sys-
> tem of gender roles, while black children, especially in working-class
> families, are culturally conditioned to emphasize age and birth order.
> Consequently, white children are expected to display either aggressive-
> ness or passivity, nonconformity ... depending on their sex ... accord-
> ing to ethnic cultural dictates; black children are expected to be
> assertive, nonconforming, independent, nurturing regardless of their
> sex [p. 99].

In understanding the black woman it is not her culture alone or
how she is socialized that can totally account for her overrepresentation in the prison population. As Lewis (1981) states, and this writer
agrees, it is "the dominant society's reaction to them" (p. 99). It is also
how society reacts to racism and sexism, on which Lewis focuses her
final analyses. Several studies that describe the effect of racial bias on
black women are cited in Lewis's article (Bell, 1973; Owens and Bell,
1977; Owens, 1980).

Additional research shows racial implications similar to those
cited by Lewis. One of these studies is the 16-year research (1959–1974)
of 1,163 women admitted to Missouri State Correctional Facility (Foley
and Rasche, 1979). Racial biases were reported to be particularly apparent in certain aspects of their study findings. For example, the study
found that

> sentence length for all offenses, combined, showed no significant
> differences between black and white female sentences' length, but
> black women did receive longer sentences (55.1 months) than white
> women (52.5 months) and they also found that ... white women
> imprisoned for murder served one-third less than did black women
> who committed the same offense [Mann, 1988, p. 99].

Could this kind of apparent disparity in the criminal justice system be the result of all-white parole boards or altercations of black
women with primarily white prison officials, which result in additional
time? Or is this pure and simple racism in our prosecution and sentencing of black women? In chapter 10 I further report on African
American women prisoners in the court system.

Another study by Candace Kruttschnitt (1979) attempted to
identify social variables—wealth, race, prior criminal history, economic
dependency, employment, marital status, and relational distance
between the victim and offender—that predict the severity of the
disposition of 1,000 women in a county of California. The analysis

indicated that black women received more severe court dispositions than white women. Similarly, Carol Spencer and John Berocochea (1979) also found that in California parole violations, black women were reincarcerated for rule violations while white women who violated the same rules were not. It was their contention that the parole officers or agents reacted more to the black woman's race in making the decision to revoke her privileges. When you combine racism with sexism, the fate of black women in the criminal justice system is further compounded.

Stuart Adams's (1975) study "The Black-Shift Phenomenon" notes that in Washington, D.C. (sometimes referred to as Chocolate City because of its large African American population) black women appeared to be more severely penalized in the courts. In this comparison he found that of the adult female population of Washington 63 percent were black and 37 percent were white, yet the proportion of first booking into detention was 73 percent black and 27 percent white (Mann, 1988, p. 99), with 83 percent black and 17 percent white returning to jail after the initial court hearing and 97 percent of blacks given sentences for three months or longer, while only 3 percent of their white female counterparts received three months or more (Adams, 1975, p. 193).

Over time it is possible to see that the previously mentioned research has uncovered recurring variables that might in part account for the overrepresentation of blacks in the prison system. Some of the most common variables that are noted in the previous discussion are depicted in the author's "Wheel of Misfortune" (Figure 2.1).

Figure 2.1 Model: Wheel of Misfortune

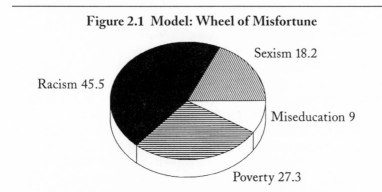

Sexism 18.2

Racism 45.5

Miseducation 9

Poverty 27.3

Source: Values assigned are based on Collins's research. See French, Mandle, Lewis, and U.S. Department of Justice, 1991 survey.

This model attempts to demonstrate that there are a number of variables that society, in some instances, continues to inflict on black women.

Black Criminology

In another interesting article, "Development of a Black Criminology and the Role of the Black Criminologist" (Russell 1992), Russell posits that the "discipline of criminology has failed ... to provide a well-developed, vibrant and cohesive subfield that seeks to explain crime committed by blacks—what is termed a 'black criminology'" (p. 667). In her article she further notes that there are studies that examine black criminology, but these are neither comprehensive nor cohesive (p. 666). This same body of literature that she spoke and wrote about is even more fragmented as it relates to female black criminology. Russell calls for the development of a black criminology "that will enable the discipline to go beyond the simple observation of a phenomenon—that blacks are disproportionately involved in crime—and will encourage the testing of new paradigms to explain the race-crime relationship" (p. 668). As she reviews the existing literature to support her call for a study in black criminology, it is obvious that most of the research that was done did not look at the development of theory to seek and explain black criminology, but rather how the criminal justice system impacts on blacks. As previously mentioned, the theoretical research regarding female criminology in general and black female criminology in particular is pitifully lacking in the literature. Most research on blacks has been directed toward the black male. Most research that attempted to explain this criminology has, as Russell explained, addressed the impact of the criminal justice system on blacks in a comparative manner (that is, black versus white crime) and based the methodology on established theories rather than investigation in the establishment of new theories. Russell (1992) sees the value in a black criminology. She concludes that there are undeveloped paradigms that present an incomplete picture of how to explain black crime.

A black criminology could, perhaps, parallel the area many posit to be a feminist criminology: which may provide a framework for developing and testing new theories (p. 681). She further notes the need to have black criminologists involved in the development of these theories, but with the scarcity of these researchers mean that contributions of others not culturally or ethnically tied to the race of the majority of the females would be required.

Male and Female Theories of Criminology

There are several other theories in the literature that attempt in general to explain the overrepresentation of minorities in the prison system. These theories are presented because they have been applied to both male and female minorities. Further, they are needed to help the reader to see the complexity of theory development. They are as follows:

1. *Labeling Theory*, which posits that people tend to perform or act like those who are watching them. In other words, their actions are controlled by what others expect them to do.

2. *Critical Theory* views crime as an element of the "capitalist mode of production, whereby all classes engaged in crime are treated differently by the system of criminal justice. According to this theory, racial differences in criminality are explicated in terms of the historically conditioned relation of different ethnic groups to the means of production" (Flowers, 1990, p. 71).

3. *Broken Home Theory* states that where parents and guardians of children are absent from the family, the children are left alone and unsupervised, which may lead to delinquency and crime.

4. *Historical Oppression Theory* contends that, due to the oppression of certain ethnic groups by racism, discrimination, or victimization, these factors "have had a cause-and-effect role in crime" (Flowers, 1990, p. 102).

5. *Genetic Inferiority Theory* simply states that you are inferior if your IQ is low. It is this low IQ that will cause a person to buy a weapon and commit a crime.

Like other theories, they fail to account for the interrelatedness of other variables that may also impact and influence an individual's participation in crime. These theories also measure minorities by norms established by and for Anglo-Americans, and any deviation from these predetermined norms result in labeling the individual or group of minorities as abnormal. Most theories have ignored ethnic customs or values or culture and their impact on decision making.

Genetics and Crime:
Concerns Regarding Racial Differences

In May 1992 the National Institute of Health awarded a grant to support the development and presentation of a conference, "Genetic Factors in Crime: Findings, Uses, and Implications." The organizers of the conference have denied that there would have been any attempt to mislead the public into thinking that criminal behavior was linked in some fashion to racial differences. With the largest population behind prison bars being African Americans, in all honesty, how could the researchers not focus their attention on this population? Another danger of this type of conference is that the presenters will primarily be white males, whose frame of reference—in some cases—will not allow them to look at the complex and critical role that environmental, sexual, and racial variables play in explaining crime. Their focus would likely have been purely on genetic differences. However, the conference has been placed on hold. In addition, the National Institute of Mental Health (NIMH) has, through its violence initiative, begun to plan and target inner-city youth for treatment because of predictions that this group will become violent.

In conclusion, theories of female criminality had their unfortunate birth in the mind of several white male researchers, who were more interested in uncovering physical or sexual abnormality to support their blatant and sexist hypotheses. It was not until the late 1930s and early 1940s that some investigators began to notice the large number of black women in the prison population. This recognition prompted a series of investigative studies that were primarily comparative, first male to female and later white female to black female offenders. These female comparative studies borrowed and utilized methods designed for male-centered research. As these theories of female criminality emerged and were applied to black female offenders, they failed to provide empirical data to support a valid theory of African American female criminality. Noting the lack of African American criminologists, the social, environmental, and cultural significance of research may have been overlooked or not considered important when studying this population. Once again in the 1990s there has been a resurgence of interest in genetic differences that may be racially motivated by those who seek a genetic difference to explain a very complex issue. Thus, there have been many fragmented attempts to address

African American female criminality by investigating arrest records, racism, sexism, poverty, demographics, and social and environmental influences.

All of these variables are important, demonstrating the complexity of the issue surrounding a theory of African American female criminality and the overrepresentation of this group in the prison population.

Chapter 3

Correctional Data and Survey Findings

Historical and Current Data Presentation
Regarding the Disparity in Corrections Statistics

Statistical information can be used to convince your audience of the validity of your views. Statistics can also be used to shape the truth in such a manner that public opinion is affected. Further, incomplete data can also be used to keep the truth from being told. In this author's analysis of historical, published correctional data regarding African American female prisoners, it was apparent that data of trends over time, upon which conclusions can be drawn, are inconsistent or completely absent. For example, in some years data by sex and race are presented, but in other years the data presented were for males and females with race omitted. Therefore, no rational conclusion can be drawn. Were these omissions deliberate or were the statisticians unaware of what data might be needed by future researchers and others concerned about women prisoners? In order to gain a clear picture regarding overrepresentation of African American women in prison facilities, it was necessary to review historical data in order to help explain the current disparities in the incarceration of African American females.

In Search of Historical Data
on African American Female Prisoners

Statistics regarding specific characteristics of a given population are usually drawn from the records of agencies that have an interest in or are designated as the collectors or depositories of this information. When you attempt to identify various sources of data on African American females, their importance is evident by the scarcity of data regarding them: the expendable masses.

Nevertheless, there is some limited historical evidence in an 1890 census report that appears to be the government's first attempt to collect data by the race of inmates (U.S. Department of Commerce Catalog of U.S. Census Population p. 20, 1974). However, these initial data did have several shortcomings in that they did not define terms used, such as convict or prisoners. Therefore, the data could not be used in a comparative manner with future reports. From 1880 to 1910 this report went through numerous revisions that resulted in the identification of the facilities that reported the information as well as the age, sex, and race of its prison population. In 1886 the Justice Department was mandated to collect yearly statistics on federal prisoners. In 1946 the Census Bureau discontinued reporting this data and the Bureau of Justice assumed this collection role. Since that time, the Bureau of Prisons has collected and reported prison data in several reports: Federal Bureau of Prisons (1946–70); Law Enforcement Assistance (1977–79); and Bureau of Justice Statistics (1980–). The Bureau of Prisons also publishes several other documents that serve as resources for this chapter (Bureau of Justice Statistical Annual Report and Prisoners in State and Federal Institutions). In another report—worth mentioning because of its shortcomings—Historical Correction Statistics in the United States 1850–1984 (U.S. Department of Justice, Bureau of Justice Statistics, 1986) only reported the percentage of females in jail and omitted all other comparative data.

One of the more factual and complete sets of data regarding African American female prisoners was found in the Uniform Crime Report published by the Federal Bureau of Investigation. Although this document contained some useful information, there were major problems with some of its data. Because the FBI served only as the depositor of data for local law enforcement agencies, there were no strict enforcement guidelines for the way in which data were to be reported. As a result, law enforcement agencies volunteered to submit their prisoners' data that were often late or they failed to report at all. Therefore, it is impossible to analyze these historical data, because they contained gaps for longitudinal comparative purposes. These data inconsistencies are noted in the writings of Ronald Flowers (1989), who stated the following:

> ... Uniform Crime Report, there are serious deficiencies in their methodology and data. One of the most critical is the inconsistency of crime reporting from one police department to the next and ... the prison population may indicate more about the differential enforcement of law, race, social class, and other biases, than crime itself. Also, as in other sources of crime data, prisoners statistics and self reports are subject to methodological problems, honesty, voluntary cooperation, non-validation and incompatibility with other statistical sources—all of which further limit their accuracy as measurements of crime and criminals [pp. 4, 10].

The noted inconsistencies and omissions in published government documents, and the long-term effects of these omissions has led to speculation as to why this was allowed to exist. With incomplete and scarce data regarding the characteristics of African American female prisoners, the author developed a survey questionnaire that was sent in 1992 to all state and federal prison officials. The results of this Collins Survey, the American Correctional Association (ACA) Report, *The Female Offender: What Does the Future Hold?* (1990), several Bureau of Prisons reports, and other data sources are presented below.

Growth in the Prison Population

There has been an unprecedented growth in the number of inmates in federal and state correctional facilities. Some attribute this growth to the so-called "1980 war on drugs." I call it "no 1980 war on poverty, unemployment, racism, miseducation, and sexism." This surge of inmates into state and federal prisons resulted in a growth over a ten-year period (1980–90) from 13,420 to 44,234 (Price and Sokoloff, 1995, p. 6). In order to accurately ascertain how large this growth was for African American females, two national surveys were conducted or requested. The first survey, conducted in 1991 and 1992 by this author, was of state facilities that housed female inmates. The second survey was requested in 1991, 1992 and 1996 by the Bureau of Prisons, Office of Research and Evaluation,* on federal female inmates. In addition, other data sources that provided some evidence to the growth of the female prison population included the American Correctional Association Report and *Vital Statistics in Corrections.*

The Bureau of Prisons Office of Research and Evaluation responded to a survey questionnaire prepared by the author.

Table 3.1 Female State Prison Population
by Race and Region, 1880–1904, in Percentages*

	1880		1923		1904	
	W	B	W	B	W	B
Northeast	93.0	7.0	84.6	15.4	81.8	18.2
Midwest	71.0	29.0	78.0	22.0	51.6	48.4
South	14.2	85.8	20.4	79.6	9.8	90.2
West	80.0	20.0	90.0	10.0	73.9	26.1

Source: Prepared from data in *Partial Justice: Women in State Prisons 1800–1935* (p. 142) by Nicole Hahn Rafter. Copyright 1985 by Nicole Hahn Rafter. Used with permission of Northeastern University Press, Boston.

Historical Comparative Data

Historical data for trends over time, as previously mentioned, contained omissions and inconsistencies when attempting to determine the specific number of African American females who were in state and federal prisons and jails. For example, in two federal documents in the years 1925 and 1986, data on prisoners admitted to state and federal institutions and historical statistics on prisoners in state and federal institutions include race but omit gender. Therefore, trends over time cannot be constructed.

In her book *Partial Justice: Women in State Prisons 1800–1935*, Nicole Rafter provides some limited trend data. She cites prison populations for the years 1880, 1904, and 1923 by percentage and regional location of incarceration (see Table 3.1).

As previously noted, following the Emancipation Proclamation and further supported by Rafter's data, African American women were herded into Southern prisons in record numbers. More data found in *Vital Statistics in Corrections* and presented in Figure 3.1 further illustrate the continued growth (1985 and 1988) in the adult African American prison population. Particularly dramatic growth is apparent in the African American and Hispanic female inmate population.

This report does not make a distinction in terms of facility type. Rather it is titled under the general term of "institutions." In 1979 the Government Accounting Office reported the ethnic female prison population. Their accounting was based on a percent of prison population as compared to women in the general female population (see Table 3.2).

Figure 3.1 Adult Female Inmate Population
by Ethnicity and Race, 1983, 1988

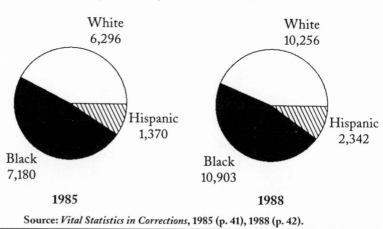

Source: *Vital Statistics in Corrections*, 1985 (p. 41), 1988 (p. 42).

Table 3.2 Female Inmates
in State and Federal Prisons as Compared to
Females in the General Population, 1978, in Percentages

	In Prison	General Population
White	35.7	82.0
Black	50.2	11.0
Hispanic	9.1	5.0
Native American	3.2	0.4
Other	1.8	1.6

Source: U.S. General Accounting Office, 1979, p. 8.

As indicated in the GAO study, African Americans made up 11 percent of the females in the general population, but 50.2 percent of the prison inmate population. In 1978, when compared to their white counterparts, this is an extremely significant statistic.

Federal prisons have also seen a tremendous growth in the African American female inmate population. From the early 1960s to the present, the federal African American inmate population has tripled. From the early 1970s through the Nixon and Reagan eras, when drug

Figure 3.2 Federal Female Inmates
by Race, Ethnicity, 1960–96

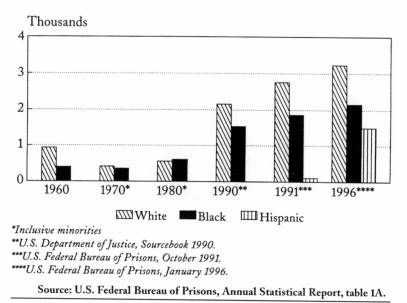

Thousands

☒ White   ■ Black   ⊞ Hispanic

*Inclusive minorities
**U.S. Department of Justice, Sourcebook 1990.
***U.S. Federal Bureau of Prisons, October 1991.
****U.S. Federal Bureau of Prisons, January 1996.

Source: U.S. Federal Bureau of Prisons, Annual Statistical Report, table 1A.

policies focused on lock-up rather than treatment and evaluation, many drug-dependent African American women found themselves in federal prisons (see Figure 3.2 and Chapter 5).

Surveys of State and Federal Prisons 1991–92

In 1991 and 1992 the author conducted a survey of state and federal correctional facilities to ascertain the actual numbers of incarcerated African American women and other minorities.

The survey questionnaire was sent to all correctional facilities that housed female inmates. In all, 50 facilities responded.* One problem experienced in the analyses of state prisons data was that 12 facilities reported a total number of female inmates only, while the remaining 36 facilities reported totals by race. Therefore, the data from those 12 facilities (totaling 5,928) have been excluded in Figure 3.3. Figure 3.3 represents a total of 36 state facilities that responded to the question, "How many female inmates by race/ethnicity are housed in your facility?"

*Not all state prisons reported and some replies were disregarded because of errors.

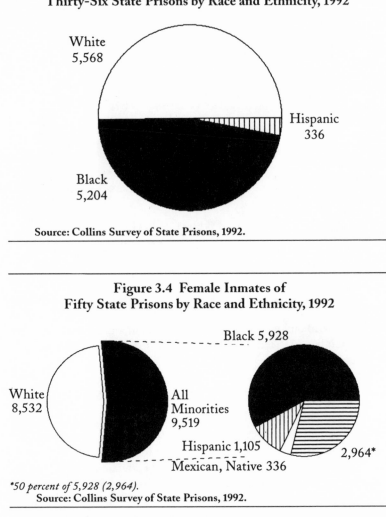

**Figure 3.3 Female Inmates of
Thirty-Six State Prisons by Race and Ethnicity, 1992**

White
5,568

Hispanic
336

Black
5,204

Source: Collins Survey of State Prisons, 1992.

**Figure 3.4 Female Inmates of
Fifty State Prisons by Race and Ethnicity, 1992**

Black 5,928

White
8,532

All
Minorities
9,519

Hispanic 1,105

2,964*

Mexican, Native 336

*50 percent of 5,928 (2,964).
Source: Collins Survey of State Prisons, 1992.

When all data from the 50 reporting facilities are totaled, there are 18,051 female inmates in state prisons (see Figure 3.4). If you further combine 1,015 Hispanics, 336 Mexicans and Native Americans, 5,204 African Americans, and a modest 50 percent (2,964) of the total of the 12 facilities that reported, Figure 3.4 depicts another dramatic increase in minority female prisoners.

Figure 3.5 New York State
Female Prisoners by Race and Ethnicity, 1992

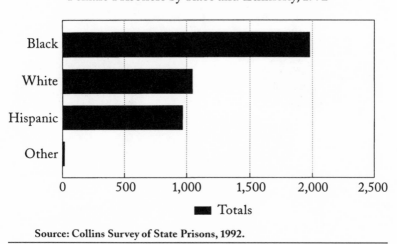

■ Totals

Source: Collins Survey of State Prisons, 1992.

Figure 3.6 New York State Inmates:
Race, Ethnicity Trends, 1985–92

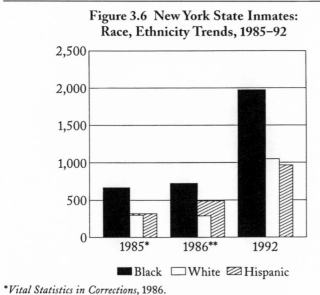

■ Black   ☐ White   ▨ Hispanic

Vital Statistics in Corrections, 1986.
**Vital Statistics in Corrections*, 1989.

Source: Collins Survey of State Prisons, 1992.

Figure 3.7 Federal Female Inmate Population 1970, 1980

Other
360

Other
619

White
411

White
567

1970

1980

Source: U.S. Federal Bureau of Prisons, Research and Evaluation, 1991 Annual Report, 1970–1980, Table A-3.

Figure 3.7A Federal Female Inmate Population, 1960

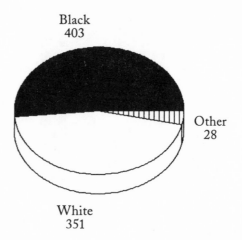

Black
403

Other
28

White
351

Source: U.S. Census Population, Subject Report: Inmates of Institutions, Final Report, 1960, PCC2-8A, p. 21).

Since the New York State correctional facilities comprise the third largest correctional system in the United States; has a significant number (2,946) of ethnic minority female prisoners (see Figure 3.5); has one of the largest prison expansion building programs; and the death penalty has been reinstated by Governor Pataki, this state's facilities have been selected for further analysis.

New York State reported 2,946 minority inmates. According to the Collins Survey, in rank order, the states with the highest number of female inmates were as follows: New York State, 4,002; California, 1,700; Ohio Reformatory, 1,411; and Gatesville, Texas, 1,759. The lowest was New Hampshire with 13 female inmates. In comparing the Collins 1992 New York State ethnic and racial inmate population figures with previous reported years—*Vital Statistics in Corrections* (1985–88)—there is a noticeably dramatic increase in incarcerated African American women (see Figure 3.6). In a seven-year period, the African American female population in New York State Correctional Facilities tripled.

Female Inmate Population of Federal Prisons

Like that of the state correctional facilities' population, federal female prison population has also experienced a significant growth in the number of African American prisoners. The U.S. Department of Justice, Federal Bureau of Prisons (Office of Research and Evaluation) responded to a 1991 request for comparative data for 1970 and 1980 of its female inmate population by facility and location. Responses to the Collins Survey request indicated that the bureau records combined ethnic and racial data into two categories: white and others. Apparently, the "other" category was used as a catchall for imprisoned African Americans, Hispanics, Native Americans, and other nonwhite female inmates (see Figure 3.7). However, in an earlier published report (U.S. Census Population, Subject Report: Inmates of Institutions, Final Report, 1960, PC (2-8A, p. 21) data, are listed by native or foreign born, white, black and other races (see Figure 3.7A). Once again, comparative trend data are difficult to analyze or ascertain from government documents.

The Bureau of Prisons also was able to provide racial and ethnic data for more current years (see Figure 3.8).

Even though the number of white inmates outnumber the African

Figure 3.8 Female Inmates of
Federal Prisons, 1991, 1992 and 1996

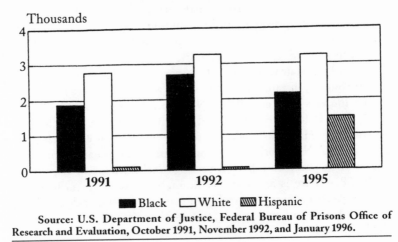

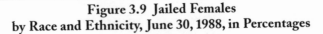

Source: U.S. Department of Justice, Federal Bureau of Prisons Office of
Research and Evaluation, October 1991, November 1992, and January 1996.

Figure 3.9 Jailed Females
by Race and Ethnicity, June 30, 1988, in Percentages

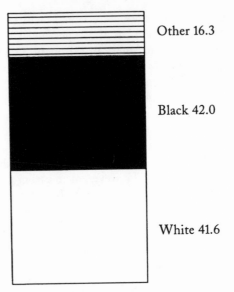

Other 16.3

Black 42.0

White 41.6

Source: U.S. Department of Justice, Sourcebook 1990.

Figure 3.9A Female Inmates in Jail
by Region, Race, and Ethnicity, June 30, 1988

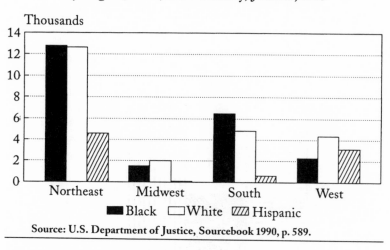

Source: U.S. Department of Justice, Sourcebook 1990, p. 589.

American inmates, we must always keep in mind that African Americans make up only 11 percent of the U.S. population.

Jailed African American Females

In 1988 the characteristics of women in local jails closely mirrored the state prison female population. They were mostly black, poor, uneducated, and mothers of small children, but their crimes were predominantly misdemeanors such as drug abuse and prostitution. Local jails are the bottomless pits where women are abused from intake—they are patted down, strip searched for narcotics including buttocks, anus, and vagina, and often sexually abused by other prisoners and male guards. (See the 1995 and 1996 Amy Fisher report of an alleged rape by a correctional officer.) In June 1988 a one-day survey of jails throughout the nation revealed a jailed population that was primarily people of color (see Figure 3.9). In addition, most of these African American females were housed in the Northeast region (see Figure 3.9A) as were their white female counterparts.

Health of Jailed Females

More often than not, female inmates come into the criminal justice system with multiple health conditions. A study by the American

**Figure 3.10 Average Percentage of
Inmates Who Are Pregnant at Intake**

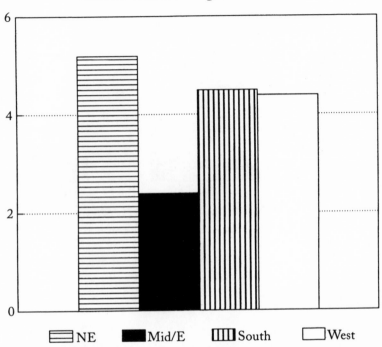

Source: Reprinted from ACA, *The Female Offender: What Does the Future Hold?*
1990, p. 17, with permission of American Correctional Association, Laurel, MD.

Correctional Association (ACA) exposed many of these health problems
in their survey of 200 jails. In this report (1990) many of the female
prisoners were often pregnant and lived in the Northeast (see Figure
3.10; also see Chapter 9 for more current data on pregnancy).

The American Correctional Association reported that these
women also have some form of disability, such as a learning disability
(LD), or are emotionally disturbed (ED), severely mentally retarded
(SMR), or have a combination of disabilities (COD) (see Figure 3.11).

Most jails housing the largest numbers of females in 1983, in
descending order, were in the South followed by the West, Northcen-
tral, and then the Northeast (Flowers, 1987, p. 161). In 1988 the incarceration of females by region had not changed, with the South maintaining the lead in housing the largest number of African Americans
and other minorities (see Figure 3.12).

Figure 3.11 Percentage of Female Inmates with a Disability

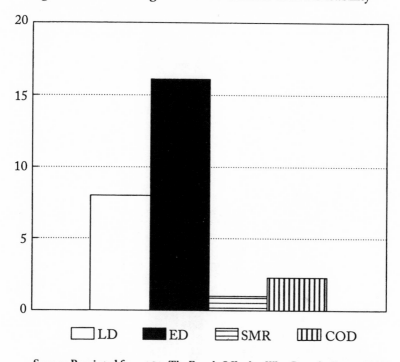

Source: Reprinted from ACA, *The Female Offender: What Does the Future Hold?*
1990, p. 18, with permission of American Correctional Association, Laurel, MD.

Federal Prison Expansion

According to the General Accounting Office's May 1992 Prison
Expansion Report, there is an unprecedented number of new and existing prison expansions underway. The following information is cited in
the report: "[The] Bureau of Prison budget plans as of May 1991 include
6 new facilities to open in 1992, 13 in 1993, 14 in 1994, and 14 in 1995
for a total of 47 new prison facilities.... Also planned are 16 expansion
efforts to include 6 expansions in 1992, 9 in 1993, and 1 in 1994" (p. 1).

These expansions and building programs are being planned to
house more than 98,000 inmates by 1995, with an institutional increase
by 70 percent (from 68 percent in 1991) to 115 institutions by 1995. This
report does not specifically mention the number of facilities planned

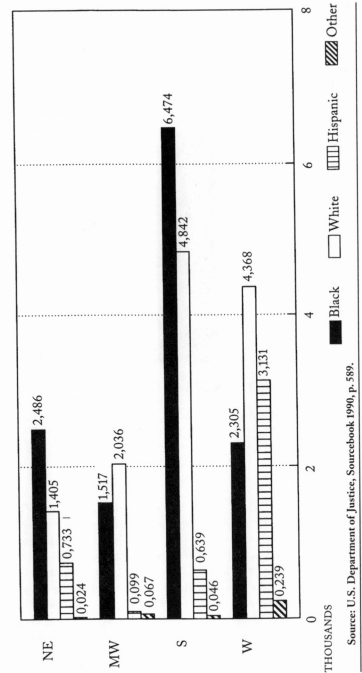

Figure 3.12 Inmates in Jail by Race, Ethnicity, and Region, 1988

Black ☐ White ⊞ Hispanic ▨ Other

THOUSANDS

Source: U.S. Department of Justice, Sourcebook 1990, p. 589.

Figure 3.13 New and Additional
Prison Facilities for Women, in Percentages

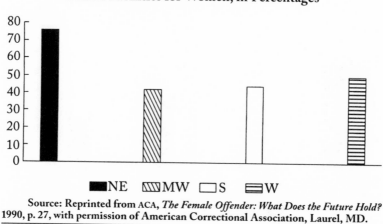

■NE ⬚MW ☐S ⬚W

Source: Reprinted from ACA, *The Female Offender: What Does the Future Hold?*
1990, p. 27, with permission of American Correctional Association, Laurel, MD.

for women. However, as of November 1992 there were 14 federal female facilities housing the following female inmates: 2,093 black, 3,268 white, and 705 others. In January 1996 there were 21 federal women's facilities housing 2,154 blacks, 3,234 whites, 1,496 Hispanics, 112 Asians, 54 Native Americans, and 737 others (U.S. Department of Justice, correspondence 1996).

State Prison Expansion

In the 1990 survey report by the American Correctional Association there is also cited an unprecedented expansion program within the Northeast, the region of the country with the most aggressive new prison plan (see Figure 3.13).

In addition, the majority of these new prisons are a combination of maximum (max), medium (med), and minimum (min) security facilities and all are primarily located in the Northeast (see Figure 3.14).

Jail Expansion

In its 1990 survey the American Correctional Association states that this nation has also developed a very aggressive jail expansion program, and the "national average, 42.8 percent of the jurisdictions are planning to build new or additional facilities for women inmates" (p. 12; see Figure 3.15).

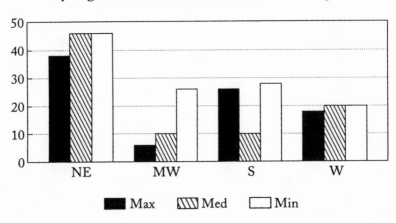

Figure 3.14 New Facilities
by Region and Classification, 1990, in Percentages

Source: Reprinted from ACA, *The Female Offender: What Does the Future Hold?*, 1990, p. 27, with permission from the American Correctional Association.

Figure 3.15 New or Additional
Facilities for Female Inmates, in Percentages

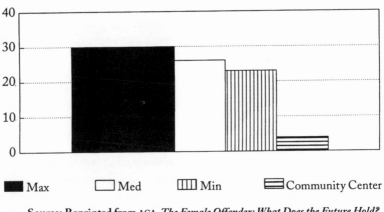

Source: Reprinted from ACA, *The Female Offender: What Does the Future Hold?*, 1990, p. 12, with permission from the American Correctional Association.

In 1994 the federal government budgeted billions of dollars for prison expansions, and 100,000 new police officer positions (see Chapter 8). Unfortunately, a nationwide prison expansion appears to be the only creative approach that law enforcement agencies and legislative bodies have to respond to our nation's social ills: drugs, AIDS, mental health problems, miseducation, racism, unemployment, homelessness, and sexism. Or this expansion program could be geared to coincide with the Department of Justice's new, innovative $23 million Weed and Seed Program. This program is designed to weed the community of gangs and seed it with new programs. The weeds will more than likely be African Americans and Hispanics who currently swell our prison cells. A discussion of Weed and Seed is not included in this book. In my review of this program, there appears to be a shifting of resources rather than actual new initiatives. For this reason, the Crime Bill Ounce of Prevention Program appears to be the source of new money and is presented in Chapter 8.

Prisons and jails, two of our nation's oldest institutions, may very well always be a part of our community and necessary for those who commit crimes. But clearly the overrepresentation of African Americans and other minority females housed in these institutions leads one to believe that there are forces within our social and criminal justice system that severely penalize women for being first a woman, second a minority, third poor, fourth uneducated, and fifth for having the audacity to come before the courts and expect justice. The data presented clearly depict these women as victims of our society, where equal access to education, employment, housing, and health care leaves them vulnerable and trapped in the wheel of misfortune, to which the author has arbitrarily assigned values (which have no statistical base) based on her review of the literature, visits to U.S. courts, and living as an African American female.

Chapter 4

Crimes Committed by African American Females

African American are incarcerated in record numbers in U.S. jails, both state and federal prisons. Are the crimes they commit more serious than their white or Hispanic cell mates, or are they just victims of their poor neighborhoods and a biased court system? In their communities poverty and drugs pit sister against sister, resulting in hatred turned inward and then unleashed on the ones closest to them, as evidenced by black on black crime. These fallen victims (for example, boyfriends and children) get the brunt of this anger and despair. For example, in 1986 for all blacks in the age group 15–35 homicide was the leading cause of death. In that same year 19 out of every 1,000 African American women were murdered and every four hours a woman was a victim of domestic violence (Avery, 1990, p. 37).

African American women are often born into poverty and continue to live in poverty, a situation that provides the impetus for many to enter into prostitution and the overwhelming obstacle in their ability to leave the streets. Relegated to a life of entrapment by poverty, they are now perceived as a major threat to society by spreading the AIDS virus. Most of these streetwise prostitutes engage primarily in lower-risk sexual acts, such as oral-genital and manual masturbation (Blumberg, 1989; Decker, 1987; Goldsmith, 1993). Street prostitutes, who make up about 20 percent of all commercial sex workers (Goldsmith, 1993; De Zalduondo, 1991), are indeed more likely to contract the AIDS virus from the john who refuses to use condoms and backs this up by threatening to expose the females as prostitutes.

In theory, law enforcement personnel are supposed to protect all citizens; however, racism and sexism directed toward African American

Figure 4.1 Crimes Committed
by Female Inmates of Federal Prisons, by Race, 1992

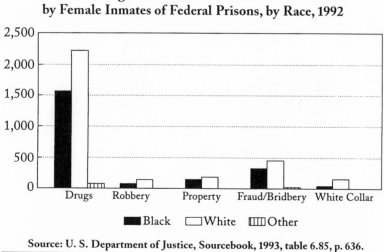

Black   White   Other

Source: U. S. Department of Justice, *Sourcebook*, 1993, table 6.85, p. 636.

Figure 4.2 Deadly Crimes Committed
by Female Inmates of State Prisons, by Race, 1986

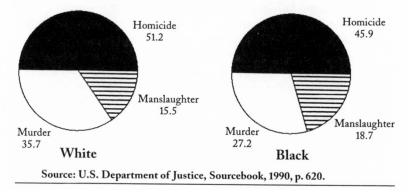

Source: U.S. Department of Justice, *Sourcebook*, 1990, p. 620.

female prostitutes protect the john, who more often than not is an upper middle-class suburban white male. Therefore, African American female prostitutes, as noted by Flowers, are seven times more likely to be arrested for prostitution than women of other races or ethnic groups (1987, p. 129). When poverty traps African American women into a life of street servitude, their crimes are closely tied to economic

**Figure 4.3 Less Violent Crimes Committed
by Female Inmates of State Prisons, by Race, 1986**

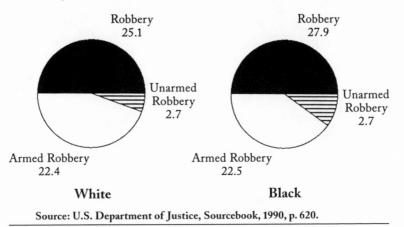

Robbery
25.1

Robbery
27.9

Unarmed
Robbery
2.7

Unarmed
Robbery
2.7

Armed Robbery
22.4

Armed Robbery
22.5

White   **Black**

Source: U.S. Department of Justice, Sourcebook, 1990, p. 620.

factors. As noted in Figure 4.1, among those federal crimes most often committed by African American women economic or monetary motivated factors are the most glaring cause.

As indicated in Figure 4.2, with the exception of slight differences (15.5 versus 18.7), white women in state prison systems committed more deadly crimes than their African American counterparts.

Another look at less violent crimes indicates that African American women inmates have a slight edge over their white cellmates (see Figure 4.3). The crimes associated with streetwalkers are robbery of the wealthy, middle-class suburban white male johns. Therefore, it is not surprising to see the increase in the number of women in state prisons.

Also associated with street prostitutes are assaults by johns, other prostitutes, and police officers. In these categories, assaults are characteristic of life on the street (see Figure 4.4).

As previously mentioned, data collected by governmental agencies are not consistent from year to year. For example, in an effort to update data previously presented in figures 4.4 and 4.5, comparison data for violent crimes committed in 1991 and 1992 were not included in the Department of Justice sourcebooks for those years.

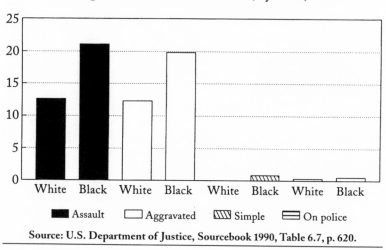

Figure 4.4 Violent Female Offenders
Serving Sentences in State Prisons, by Race, 1986

Source: U.S. Department of Justice, Sourcebook 1990, Table 6.7, p. 620.

African American Women:
Execution and Death Row

African American women are among those sentenced for execution, and between 1930 and 1967 African American females accounted for 38 percent of women put to death. Overall, the greatest number of black executions occurred in the South. This has been the apparent practice from the very early days of unlawful black lynching, which in 1890 saw 1,111 lynchings, with 162 occurring in 1892. However, the execution of blacks is what many believe to be the legal version of lynching, and this procedure has come under more scrutiny in the past several years. Another set of data shows that from 1930 to 1989 there were 33 women executed (31 for murder and 2 for kidnapping and espionage). Of those women executed, 21 were white and 12 were black. As noted by Cardess Collins:

> Time and again we have seen how African American men and women are disproportionately sentenced to death—even when one accounts for the crime committed. Since 1988, 33 of the 37 Federal death penalty defendants have been African American. In the current

administration, which I look upon as being more enlightened regarding the unfairness of our judicial system, all of the defendants the Attorney General has approved for the death penalty have been African American [*Congressional Digest*, June-July 1994, p. 181].

(See chapter 7 for more detailed discussion of this issue.)

Clearly, the quick fix for the overcrowded prison population could be to clear out some of those inmates scheduled for possible execution. Even the staunch Mario Cuomo, the former New York State governor, prior to losing the governor's election, began to shift his thinking on executions. Cuomo once felt that this punishment "brutalizes" society (*New York Times*, July 9, 1994, p. 25). Governor Pataki won the New York governship with the promise to reinstate the death penalty, which he did. New York State, which has had a very healthy prison population and budget, in 1994-95 alone provided $44 million for prison programs and the conversion of a psychiatric hospital to a 750-cell medium security prison (*New York Times*, p. 24). Are there other discriminating disparities in the use of capital punishment? According to the *Congressional Digest* 1994, "Eighty-five percent of the defendants selected for capital punishment under the Kingpin Death Provision have either been African-American or Mexican-American, despite the fact that 75 percent of those individuals convicted under the general drug kingpin statue were white" (p. 173). The majority of the executions took place in the Southern states, with the state of Mississippi leading with the most executions (U.S. Department of Justice, Office of Justice Programs, Sourcebook, 1990 Bulletin). Has the United States become more or less racist in its use of the death penalty? In the debate over the Violent Crime Control and Law Enforcement Act of 1994 (Crime Bill) there were over 50 new federal offenses that were punishable by the death penalty. The Racial Justice Act, which may have released a number of innocent people from execution, was removed from the legislation (see Chapter 8). Further, it has always been the opinion of many in the African American community that whites favor the death penalty far greater than they do. In an article by Steven Barkan and Steven Cohn (1994) they reported on "whether whites' support for the death penalty is, in fact, associated with racial prejudice." It uses data from the 1990 General Social Survey (GSS) (Davis and Smith), which included a special module of items on racial attitudes and perceptions (Barkan and Cohn, 1994, p. 203). The results of the study indicated that "white support for the death penalty is, as hypothesized, associated

with antipathy to blacks and with racial stereotyping," and that "southern whites are also slightly more supportive" (p. 205). The study concluded that white support for the death penalty was associated with
racial prejudice (p. 206), a further indication of the need to have
included the Racial Justice Act of 1994 in the Crime Bill. Further, a
poll released by the Quinnipiac College in Hamden, Connecticut, indicated that 44 percent of New York residents supported a life sentence
in prison without parole, but only 40 percent supported capital punishment (*New York Times*, July 9, 1994, p. 25). Can we expect African
American prisoners to receive a fair trial and appropriate sentencing
with these kind of prejudicial and racist attitudes permeating our U.S.
social-class structure?

An example of this lack of fairness is the Joyce Brown case, an
African American female who was accused of armed robbery and murder in the state of Texas. She was falsely accused by the police, who
did not follow up on evidence that would have cleared her. She was also
accused by a jail-house snitch, who said Brown admitted to the crime.
Brown was to serve 20 years before being eligible for parole. She served
9 years and 24 days before being freed (*Geraldo*, "Want to Do a Crime—
Blame a Black Man," January 24, 1995).

Behind the Prison Wall: The Protectors

Once African American women enter the criminal justice system, their victimization does not stop there. As discussed earlier, there
has been a continual stream of cases of mistreatment and sexual
exploitation by prison guards and other female inmates. A recent example of the mistreatment of female inmates was reported to have
occurred in Albion correctional facility in New York State. You may
recall the story of Amy Fisher, the 16-year-old Long Island resident
who shot Mary Jo Buttafuoco, her supposed lover's wife. Fisher says,
"I was raped by a prison guard, abused by correctional staff and beaten
by inmates since going to prison" (*Buffalo News*, January 19, 1995). A
case of a black women that received national attention was that of
Joanne Little. She had been arrested and jailed in 1974 in Beaufort
County, North Carolina. While she sat for three months waiting for
an appeal on a larceny conviction, she was made to have oral sex with
a white 62-year-old jailer. After an argument, the jailer was found in
her cell nude from the waist down. He had clearly emitted seminal fluid

prior to his death by stabbing with an ice pick. Little was charged but later freed after a change of venue trial, along with support from civil rights organizations, feminists, and advocates of prison reform (Little, 1975).

Female matrons initially came into correctional services to prevent the exploitation of female prisoners. In many of these early prisons male prison guards would rape or force the women into prostitution. As reported by Estelle Freedman (1981), the prison administration in Indiana operated a prostitution service for the male guards. Female inmates were forced to provide whatever sexual favor was requested. It is no wonder that the state with this kind of recorded abuse of women inmates would be the first to open an all-female prison in 1874. However, attitudes with respect to female guards did not change much. Most men felt that women could not control a criminal, so there was still much reluctance to have them. Nevertheless, in other locations women were being hired in local jails to supervise female prisoners. Initially, the job market was not that plentiful, with only 16 states having separate prisons for women in 1975. In 1991, there were 67 state prisons for adult women in 42 states, 33 state coed facilities, and many jails and other lock-ups to house women prisoners and provide employment for female guards. However, the Civil Rights Act of 1964 helped to satisfy the demands of the women's movement, enabling females to be hired as prison guards. It hasn't been easy for women in general or black women in particular to gain employment in corrections. Once inside, female guards may be subjected to strong-arm abuse by their male coworkers, who may see them as a threat. Some feel that women jeopardize their safety because the male guards may have to defend them in case of a prison uprising, or they feel that female guards may be given other privileges once afforded to them (for example, light duty). Apparently, male inmates appreciate female officers. In some cases inmate appearance and language have improved and they behave "more politely toward the female officers" (Pollock-Byrne, 1990, p. 117). A female correctional officer reported to me that "My area was tense all day; two rival gangs were mad about something and it was a hot day. Everything was okay until I left the lock-up and the male guards came on duty. Then all hell broke out. I believe the male prisoners did not want me to get hurt. So they waited until I left."

The African American female who chooses to work in a prison environment must always be mindful that the majority of the inmates are black. She must also be mindful that, today, the majority of those

**Figure 4.5 Correctional Officers
in Adult Systems, by Sex and Race, 1985, 1990, 1993**

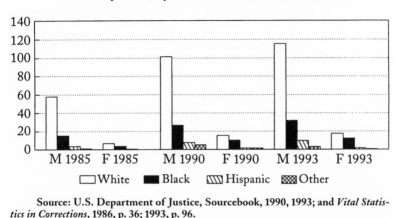

Source: U.S. Department of Justice, Sourcebook, 1990, 1993; and *Vital Statistics in Corrections*, 1986, p. 36; 1993, p. 96.

officers who are employed in the criminal justice system are white men. The prison system has become very attractive (with good benefits) for white men, the majority of employees in both state and federal facilities.

In a 1979 survey it was reported that 29.3 percent of correctional officers were female, with 41 percent having contact with female prisoners. Other female employees were clerical and support staff (Pollock-Byrne, 1990, p. 115). Not only are the majority of U.S. prisons staffed primarily with white males, the facilities are located in rural and suburban communities where other positions are also held by white rural dwellers, many of whom are insensitive and have rarely interacted with the major ethnic or racial female inmate population. In most cases these white correctional officers have been sensitized by the media, which stereotypes blacks. The numbers of prison employees, as noted in Figure 4.5, have seen a consistent increase. In the past eight years the numbers of white male officers assigned to adult correctional facilities have continued to escalate, while the numbers of black male correctional officers have increased only slightly. In general, female correctional officers have not experienced the same growth (see Figure 4.5).

Another way to look at the data regarding change in the number of African American correctional officers in the U. S. adult systems is shown in Table 4.1. White male correctional officers outnumber all ethnic or racial minorities and female correctional officers.

In New York State, which has one of the nation's largest African

Table 4.1 Correctional Officers in Adult State Systems, by Race, Sex, and Ethnicity, June 30, 1993

	Male	*Female*
White	115,443	17,527
Black	31,797	12,431
Hispanic	9,904	1,598
Other	2,867	513

Source: U.S. Department of Justice, Sourcebook 1993, Table 1.82, p. 96.

Table 4.2 New York State Correctional Officers by Race, Sex and Ethnicity, June 30, 1993

	Male	*Female*
White	16,900	903
Black	1,643	579
Hispanic	597	77
Other	102	17

Source: U.S. Department of Justice, Sourcebook 1993, Table 1.83, p. 98.

American inmate populations, correctional staff seriously lack minority and female correctional officers (see Table 4.2).

As previously mentioned, males—more specifically white males and to a lesser degree black males—are the major correctional personnel. Specific prison data for each state facility are unavailable.

In this chapter I have presented the crimes that women—more specifically African American women—commit. They are primarily crimes that are rooted in the need for resources to support their families and to decrease their poverty levels. They are crimes associated with robbery, assault, prostitution, and drugs. When these African American women enter the criminal justice system, the majority of their caretakers will be white males. There is also the ever-present threat of violence from their caretaker or from other prisoners (such as in the aforementioned case of the alleged attack on Amy Fisher). As more African American women enter the criminal justice system as correctional officers they too are also likely to experience some form of abuse (for example, verbal or sexual) within this male-dominated profession.

Chapter 5

The Children of Female African American Prisoners

In order to fully understand the serious problems for African American children when their caretaker is imprisoned, we must first gain some insight into the social and health status of these children.

Health and Social Status of African American Children

In general, African American children are the most vulnerable citizens of this nation. This vulnerability is heightened by their mother's arrest and subsequent imprisonment. In 1986, when prisons were overflowing with African American women, the social and health status of the children of these prisoners was deplorable. In *Ebony* magazine's 1986 article "Crisis of the Black Family," black children were compared to their white counterparts. This article states that black children are twice as likely to

1. Die during the first year of life;
2. Live in institutions;
3. See a parent die;
4. Suffer low birth weight; and
5. Be born prematurely;

three times as likely to

1. Be poor;
2. Have their mother die at childbirth;

   3. Live with a parent who is separated from the other parent;
   4. Be murdered between five and nine years of age;
   5. Be placed in an educable mentally retarded class; and
   6. Die at the hands of a known child abuser;

four times as likely to

   1. Be murdered before one year of age or as a teenager; and

five times as likely to

   1. Be dependent on welfare.

   Further, in 1988 more than half of all African American children (15 million children under age 18) lived with one parent. These children represent more than 50 percent of the African American childhood population living with a single parent, as compared to 19 percent of white children (Schmolling, 1992, p. 5). Equally important are the numbers of African American children living in poverty. In 1990 the poverty rate for African American children was 31.9 percent compared to 10.7 percent for whites. In the same year infants and toddlers were poorer than the rest of the population. When compared to prime adults (ages 25–64) who lived in poverty and whose rate was 8 percent, and those 65 and older whose rate was 13 percent, the rate for infants and toddlers was an astonishing 20 percent (U.S. General Accounting Office, 1994, p. 6). Still even more disturbing was the increase since 1980, which went from 1.8 million to 2.3 million children (p. 7). Poverty rates for these children correlate closely with the rates in many areas of the South and Southwest where more African American women have been herded into prison cells.
   Poverty is based on the ability (or lack thereof) to purchase those needed services to maintain adequate health status. To this end, these same African American children are also twice as likely as whites to be inadequately immunized (*USA Today*, 1993, p. 15A). Additionally, one of the most serious and devastating illnesses to impact African American children has been the AIDS epidemic. As Table 5.1 shows, the AIDS virus has had a severe effect on African American children.
   In the United States the increase in drug usage by African American women in inner-city communities has resulted in a deplorable

Table 5.1 Cases of Children with AIDS in the United States, by Race and Age, June 1996

	Black	White	Hispanic
Under 5 years	3,539	877	1,313
5–12	662	437	390
13–19	1,165	895	2,175
Total	5,366	2,209	2,175

Source: U.S. Department of Health and Human Services, Surveillance Report, Midyear Edition, Vol. 8, No. 1, p. 13.

impact on African American children, our most vulnerable U.S. citizens. Parental drug exposure has had a serious impact on children who are in foster care. Mothers of many of these children are abusing cocaine at an alarming rate. Between 1986 and 1991 cocaine abuse increased from 17 to 55 percent, respectively (U.S. General Accounting Office, April 1994, p. 2). Further, in a 1991 survey of state prison inmates by the Bureau of Justice, it was reported that women used more drugs and used them more frequently than men. This report stated that about 54 percent of women used drugs in the month before their arrest, and one in four females reported committing their offense to get money to buy drugs (p. 7). The impact of drugs on minority females was very significant. Of Hispanic women 4.6 percent reported injecting drugs, as did 42 percent white and 24 percent black women before admission to prison. The number of children affected may be underestimated because most medical personnel rely on the mother's self-reporting (as in the 1991 Survey of State Prison Inmates) of drug use, as well as other clinical tests. Furthermore, testing during birth will only detect recent drug use. Therefore, the effect on these vulnerable children, whose health status is already poor, is further compounded by placement in a foster care system.

Some of the health problems noted in the GAO (April 1994) study include behavioral problems, cardiac defects, low birth weight, and development delay (p. 10). Another result of the substance abuse has been an increase in the number of AIDS-infected infants. In Buffalo, New York, alone, there were 56 infants born to AIDS-infected mothers in 1992. These predisposing factors, coupled with maternal separation due to incarceration, have placed African American children at even greater risk. These now very vulnerable citizens, who have not developed the coping skills and defenses needed to deal with change, are now placed, if lucky, in the care of the inmate's extended family. According to the above-mentioned 1991 survey of state prisons, "three quarters of all women in prison had children.... An estimated 25,700 female inmates had more than 56,000 children under the age of 18. The racial/ethnic distribution were black—69 percent, Hispanic—72 percent, and white—62 percent" (p. 6). If the inmate's family, many of whom also live in poverty, are unable to care for the children, these youngsters become wards of the state (foster care) and their vulnerability is heightened even more.

The Impact of Maternal Separation on African American Children

African American children's vulnerability has never been a primary concern to those in charge of their destiny: white America. From the time of the birth of the first African American slave child they have been treated with disrespect (then seen as property sold into slavery), and today continue to die at alarming rates before their first birthday. The African American infant mortality rate in the United States in 1990–91 was 18 percent, with Third World countries like Malaysia (15 percent) and Kuwait (14 percent) doing better than African American infants (*USA Today*, December 1993, p. 15A).

African American children did not have a healthy start in the past and today so many external factors determine their fate. Years ago they, like all slaves, were considered to be the property of the slave owners, and thus, their value was set by their physical worth. In the case of African American children, their teeth set their value, while the mother's breasts and the father's weight were determinants of their worth. To separate the African American child from its family members was of little consequence then or now. Today, the lack of concern for the well-being of African American children is of minor consequence in the criminal justice system: evidenced by the disparity that exists between white and black sentencing patterns. Plagued by maternal substance abuse, and—if they survive a life of poverty—to be separated from the one stable force in their life can be very traumatic for a child.

The ideal nuclear family, where the mother has total child-rearing responsibilities, does not lend itself to the African American mother whose racial oppression has denied her family sufficient resources to support their needs. Fortunately, for survival of motherhood and its nurturing role, responsibilities had to be shared by the extended family members. For the children of African American prisoners, the extended family is their only hope. Of the previously mentioned 56,000 children of incarcerated women in 1991, it was reported in the Bureau of Justice Statistics Special Report that the grandparents of these children (57 percent black, 55 percent Hispanic, and 41 percent white) were the primary caretakers while the mother was imprisoned. While the biological mother is the ideal provider, without collective responsibility shared by the prisoner-mother, sisters, grandmothers, great-grandmothers, and other relatives, the survival of the inmates' African American children would not have occurred. Today more than 3.3 million children live with grandparents, a 41 percent increase since 1980 (*Good Housekeeping*, July 1994, p. 181). However, there are those African American children whose mother lacks the benefits of a grandmother or an extended family. These children are subjected to the individual state's foster care system. In the last five years alone this system—for young children under 5 years of age—has increased nationally from helping 280,000 in 1986 to trying to care for 429,000 in 1991. The three states with the largest number of children in foster care (New York, Pennsylvania, and California) also have the largest increase in numbers of incarcerated African American females (see Chapter 3). Thus it appears that the increase in the foster care population correlates with the 1986–1991 increase in female incarceration in these states. In most instances neglect, caretaker absence, or incapacity were the reasons for the placement of young children in New York and California.

In spite of the poor health and social status of African American children, there is very little written about their psychological and social conditions while their mothers are incarcerated. However, a number of studies have examined in general the impact of maternal separation on the family (Swan, 1981; Bresler and Lewis, 1983; Baunach, 1982; Datesman and Cales, 1990; Henriques 1996). Most of these studies argue that there are serious consequences when children are separated from their mother.

Erik Erikson's developmental theory posits that infancy is when children develop a sense of trust that is the basis for *all the other* relationships that children will develop during the rest of their life. This trust is developed from the "nurturing, concerned, and positive interaction that occurs between a living parent ... which is ... sensitive, consistent care they are given" (Lisner, 1983, p. 135). Patricia Lisner also cites that when infants are raised in an "inconsistent environment in which their needs are only sporadically met [they] may develop a sense of mistrust towards the world and the individuals in it" (p. 135).

There are also those who feel that children "who lack affection may manifest a greater tendency to develop self-destructive and delinquent behavior that imperils not only the child, but other people as well" (Huie, 1992, p. 23). Further, it is felt that children who fail to bond through the nurturing process may grow up without caring or feeling toward others, or even a conscience. Thus, these children, whom we entrust into the care of foster parents or extended family members, may experience bonding or nurturing deprivation. This could lead the child to crime-ridden streets, to be a prime candidate for the influences of gangs, drugs, miseducation, and the vicious wheel of misfortune.

African American Children
Affected by Their Mother's Incarceration

The number of children in jeopardy grows with every arrested or incarcerated female prisoner. According to the Center for Children of Incarcerated Parents at Pacific Oaks College in Pasadena, "the population of children of imprisoned parents has soared from 21,000 in 1978 to 1 million in 1990, and could reach 2 million by the year 2000" (Huie, 1992, p. 22). Again, of the 56,000 children of incarcerated women, 69 percent were children of African American female inmates. As you will note in Figure 5.1, the majority of the children affected in New York State by maternal separation are African American.

With the previously mentioned social and health factors facing African American children in general, the separation from the one parent, in most cases, can be devastating to the children.

In the American Correctional Association's 1990 survey of state facilities it was reported that the characteristics of the respondents (4 percent of 43,000 female inmates, or 1,720) to their survey were reasonably representative of the female prison population. Some specific characteristics that added to the study's validity included the following:

1. 57 percent were minorities between ages 25–29;
2. 62 percent lived alone with 1–3 children;
3. 48 percent of their children lived with a mother or grandmother; and
4. 37 percent had never been married.

Figure 5.1 Women with Children
in New York State Prisons, by Race and Ethnicity, 1992

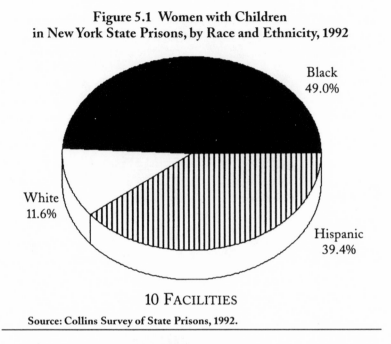

Black
49.0%

White
11.6%

Hispanic
39.4%

10 FACILITIES

Source: Collins Survey of State Prisons, 1992.

These survey results are consistent with the findings of other studies and surveys previously mentioned.

Pregnant Inmates

Pregnant inmates are entering the jailed population in what appears to be record numbers. According to the 1990 American Correctional Association study, the Northeast has the largest number of pregnant inmates on intake (Figure 5.2), while the South has the highest number of children born in prison (see Figure 5.3).

Unfortunately, the races of the study subjects—pregnant women—were omitted. However, from the data previously presented we can safely speculate that since the majority of imprisoned women are African American, they would constitute the largest number who are pregnant and give birth while incarcerated. Also at the state level, prisoners are entering at various degrees of pregnancy. In 1991, 6.1 percent

Figure 5.2 Inmates Who Are Pregnant
at the Time of Intake in Local Jails, in Percentages

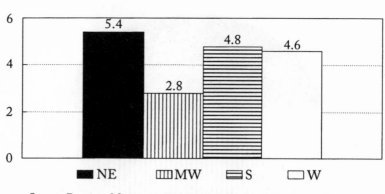

Source: Reprinted from ACA, *The Female Offender*, 1990, p. 17, with permission from the American Correctional Association.

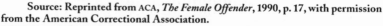

Figure 5.3 Number of Children Born to Women in Jail

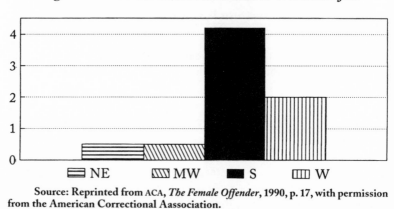

Source: Reprinted from ACA, *The Female Offender*, 1990, p. 17, with permission from the American Correctional Aassociation.

of the 25,700 inmates were pregnant at the time of admission; 5.2 percent of white, 6.7 percent of black and 5.9 percent of Hispanic inmates (U.S. Department of Justice, Bureau of Justice Statistics, Survey of State Prison Inmates, 1991, p. 10).

With her pregnancy being a major factor, the female inmate's unborn fetus is placed in serious jeopardy. The primary cause of this jeopardy can be attributed to the attitude of prison authorities who see

Table 5.2 Comparison of
Parental Services in State Facilities, 1985, 1992

	Boudouris Study 1985	*Collins Study* 1992
Prenatal classes	53	44
Furloughs	45	31
Overnight visits with children	17	14
Conjugal visits	5	9
Community facilities for mother and child	5	8
Prison nurseries	1	1

them on a regular basis: first, as unworthy of motherhood, and second, as a drain on limited prison resources, requiring such attention as special diets, vitamins, and prenatal visits.

Parental Contact with Children

The criminal justice system has been very unresponsive to the needs of its inmates' children. A survey by James Boudouris (1985) of 50 states, representing 57 institutions and 15,337 prisoners, was compared to the findings of the Collins 1992 survey of 44 states, representing 52 institutions and 14,192 incarcerated females. This comparison revealed virtually no change in parental services provided (see Table 5.2).

Certainly, there should be some attempt to satisfy the emotional and psychological needs of African American women in relation to their children. However, we have failed once again to build needed programs that will foster closer parent-child relationships. Here are a few models that are known to work:

1. Mothers and Their Children (MATCH) which provides a child-centered environment;
2. TALK program, which helps to facilitate mother-child bonding; and

3. Prisoner Mother-Infant Care program, a network of halfway houses for low-risk female prisoners and their children to live together while serving out their sentences (Huie, 1992, p. 23).

In New York State's Bedford Hill Prison, one of the few that still allow some inmates who give birth while incarcerated to keep their infant up to one year, Herman Tarnower's mistress, Jean Harris, recognized the need and established parenting classes for mothers and soon-to-be mothers. She also ran a prison program promoting more visits between inmates and their children (*Buffalo News*, October 5, 1994). It is unbelievable that a murderess—who received clemency after 12 years—and not the prison officials would have expanded existing or established additional parenting classes to meet inmates' needs; Harris saw the need and turned her skills to this prison deficiency. She is commended for this effort.

When these programs, such as those attributed to Harris's efforts, are not available for the African American female prisoner, she must draw upon one of the African American strengths: the ability to delegate and distribute the mother's role to other family members, most often the grandmother. This one custom has been the salvation for most African American children. Without the help of the extended family members, most children of prisoners would become wards of the state and be placed in the foster care system. If the mother is blessed with relatives who are willing to take on the responsibility of her children, upon release the mother can reclaim her children without too much hardship. However, if she loses her parental rights, the judicial system is unfriendly to her when she requests the return of her children. This mother must then approach a system that on one hand wants the mother to have control of her children, but on the other hand sees her as unfit and not worthy to be a mother.

No one can argue the fact that children suffer when their mother or family is unable to provide the economic resources to purchase appropriate health care. When African American mothers are separated from their children, whose health status is questionable, they are known to develop psychological behaviors similar to those encountered due to a loss through death (Flowers, 1987, p. 159). Likewise, the children have been known to experience serious psychological consequences due to the separation from the one caretaker who provides nurturing and loving support. Children who are lucky enough to be cared for by the extended family have a much better chance of being reunited once the mother is released from prison. However, very few of the children who are placed in the foster care system are returned to the mother without a struggle upon her release.

If a child is born while the mother is incarcerated, poor or no pre-natal care can severely jeopardize the health status of the unborn infant. If the infant survives the birth and reaches a certain age, the child is then separated from a mother who has in most cases bonded with the infant. When this nurturing of the prison mother is removed, once again, this vulnerable African American child is placed in jeopardy. Once again, both infant and parent experience extreme psychological disturbances.

There are many arguments, pro and con, as to why the child should not be separated from the mother. However, the judicial system has not fully explored or implemented options (for example, parole upon birth) that might better benefit both the child and the inmate mother. Nor has the system fully implemented inmate vocational and parenting classes, which help to meet the needs of those mothers who will be returning to their communities and children. If the criminal justice system does not provide opportunities for the inmate to learn while incarcerated, when she returns to a hostile, poverty-stricken environment—where it is easier to sell drugs than to get an education—she will return to prison: the ever-turning, revolving door.

Chapter 6

Prison Health

African American females who are incarcerated in jails and state facilities bring with them multiple health complaints and problems. These health problems are rooted in the way in which African American women's ancestors were socialized to view the medical profession and how the health system treated them. In the next few pages we will take a look at the historical treatment of African American women's health conditions, and the health problems of the incarcerated African American female.

Health Care for African American Women: Years of Neglect

In Edward Beardsley's article, "Race as a Factor in Health," he describes how black women were treated in three eras: Denial 1900–1930, Inclusion 1930–60, and Attempted Restitution 1960–80. This author includes one additional era: "How to Right the Wrong—1980s to present" (Beardsley, 1990).

Slave women were always viewed as personal property to do with as the slave master saw fit. For economic reasons African slaves were brought to this country. Women slaves were seen as the baby and labor maker. They were encouraged to get pregnant at the age of 15, and to have anywhere from 10 to 12 babies. The incentive for having this many babies was choice duty doing light house work or serving as a nanny for the white master's children. On one hand, the slave master saw these slave women and their babies as the key to keeping the economy moving forward and, therefore, somewhat valuable. On the other hand, these pregnant slave women and their babies were treated with the most unspeakable viciousness, as demonstrated in the following passage:

> The contempt felt about African American children and women was never so apparent as when "Mary Turner," pregnant, was hanged, and doused with gasoline as she swung by the neck. As whites watched this burning woman a man stepped forward with a pocket knife and ripped open the abdomen.... Out tumbled the prematurely born child.... Two feeble cries it gave—and received for answer the hell of a stalwart man, as life was ground out of its tiny form [Day, 1989, p. 245].

As we reached the Era of Denial, white America believed that somehow the ancestor of the African slave would disappear, because they had the least ability or fortitude to survive. This notion was the basis for their denial of medical and health services for black women. By 1914 these now very fertile black women, who were once encouraged and coerced to give birth, were giving birth and dying in childbirth at an alarming rate. A few white physicians provided limited care for these pregnant women, but like most whites they believed they were "shiftless, of low intelligence, and love[d] carnal pleasure" (Beardsley, 1990, p. 125). In other words, the reason for withholding health services was for their shiftlessness (regardless of poor housing and the lack of job opportunities), low intelligence (regardless of their having been educated, if at all, in segregated schools), and love of carnal pleasure (pregnancy being interpreted as a pleasurable state of being for women).

With these attitudes and limited health services, black women were suffering and dying from tuberculosis, venereal diseases (which also claimed the lives of many infants), and childbirth. By the mid-1930s the Social Security Act began to provide some limited maternal services for mothers and babies. However, hospitals segregated black women into large, understaffed wards, staffed by prejudiced white nurses and physicians who lacked supplies and other resources for a very sick population.

In the Era of Inclusion (1930–60) there was a glimmer of hope that some of the wrongdoings could be remedied. One of these attempts was once again made by the federal government through the Hill-Burton Act of 1947. This provided resources for the building of hospitals, not especially for blacks, but more for returning servicemen from World War II. By 1959 there were over 7,000 hospital projects completed or underway.

Figure 6.1 Lawsuits Against
Local Governments by Female Offenders

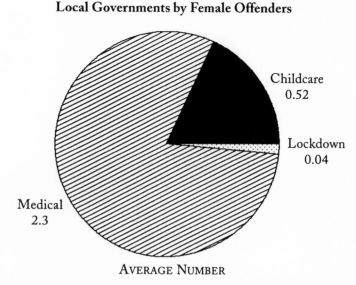

AVERAGE NUMBER

Source: Reprinted from ACA, *The Female Offender*, 1990, p. 16, with permission from the American Correctional Association.

These new hospital projects, however, continued to perpetuate an already segregated hospital system, and there was little change in attitude toward what was now America's sickest segment of the population. With the demands for equality that the civil rights and other movements posited, the Era of Attempted Restitution found the nation struggling with changing attitudes in the medical, nursing, and health professions. Pressure from the Department of Justice and other governmental interventions found the once segregated medical and nursing schools opening up enrollments and the "colored waiting room" signs were removed. However, by now the harm had been done. African American women had grown to distrust the now open system of health care. Expectant mothers had learned not to depend on white health providers, turning to untrained midwives to deliver their babies. Hospitals were now viewed as a place of last resort, and with this attitude many blacks began to seek care (often too late) in the last stages of their illness. Lifestyle behaviors that contributed to poor health habits were now embedded for the generations that followed.

Prison Health Services for Women: How to Right a Wrong

As we enter the final era of How to Right a Wrong, African American women prisoners are still experiencing the highest rate of maternal mortality, infant mortality, tuberculosis, cancer, venereal disease, and now the dreaded Acquired Immune Deficiency Syndrome (AIDS). African American female inmates come to the institutions in such deplorable health conditions that in most cases it is difficult for the prison system to provide even minimal health services. Consequently, this leads to the most lawsuits (as compared to children and lockdown) being filed against local governments during the past three years for the failure of the facility to provide adequate health services (see Figure 6.1).

The major task of most prison health services is to screen newly committed inmates to detect communicable diseases such as tuberculosis, herpes, hepatitis, AIDS, gonorrhea, and others. These health services may also include mental and physical examinations, and dental and psychological screening. All minor health complaints are handled during "sick call" where inmates' complaints of a problem are placed on a list for the next day's clinic. In some cases, though, these complaints are not heeded in time to save a person's life. Emergency care is usually provided by onsite medical personnel or in a local hospital emergency room. If an inmate needs to deliver or have other complaints requiring skilled medical and nursery care, a local hospital provides this backup resource. If a communicable disease or other medical problem is found, the inmate is usually cared for in an isolated area of the prison facility's infirmary. Dental services are handled most of the time by part-time or full-time dental personnel, depending on the size of the prison population. In the 1990 American Correctional Association report results noted that 54 percent of those reporting facilities had medical staff on site at all times, and for emergencies 23 percent were reported to transport the inmate to the local hospital (p. 102). Figure 6.2 shows the percentages of jails, as reported by the American Correctional Association, that offer various health-care services on site at least once a week.

AIDS is having a devastating impact on prison resources. Among the inmates in jail and state prison populations, the number of cases is growing with each admission, as noted in Figure 6.3. Also, see Chapter 11 for more statistics regarding AIDS in the female state inmate populations.

Figure 6.2 Health-Care Services
in Jails Nationally, in Percentages

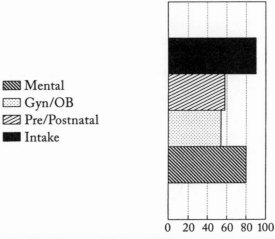

Source: Reprinted from ACA, *The Female Offender: What Does the Future Hold?*,
1990, p. 16, with permission from the American Correctional Association.

Figure 6.3 Female Inmates Who
Tested Positive for AIDS in State Prisons

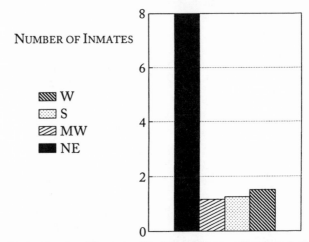

Source: Reprinted from ACA, *The Female Offender: What Does the Future Hold?*,
1990, p. 33, with permission from the American Correctional Association.

Figure 6.4 Substance Abuse at Intake
for Female Offenders in the United States, in Percentages

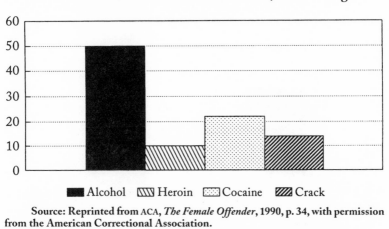

■ Alcohol ⧅ Heroin ▦ Cocaine ▨ Crack

Source: Reprinted from ACA, *The Female Offender*, 1990, p. 34, with permission from the American Correctional Association.

Nationally, as of September 1992, there were 14,792 black and 5,871 Hispanic women who were diagnosed with the AIDS virus (HIV-AIDS Surveillance Report, October 1992, p. 12).

In addition to the health conditions previously mentioned, most female inmates were also reported to need substance-abuse treatment at the time of intake. The following percentages were reported as needing treatment: for alcohol, 42.1 percent; marijuana, 46 percent; cocaine, 27 percent; crack, 16 percent; and heroin, 14 percent (American Correctional Association, 1990, p. 103). Although the race of these inmates was not reported for specific categories, the race of the 1,846 inmates in the study groups was 36 percent black and 43.4 percent white. However, in another source that confirmed inmates' drug abuse, it was stated that among the federal female inmate population 63.4 percent of the black inmates and 66 percent of the whites were confined for drug-abuse offenses (U.S. Department of Justice, Sourcebook 1990, p. 646). Drug addiction is a serious problem within the female population at intake and among jailed female offenders (see figures 6.4 and 6.5).

In addition, it is extremely difficult to get an accurate picture of the overall problem of substance abuse in the general population or society of the United States. However, a study by the National Institute on Drug Abuse (NIDA, February 1990), with regard to the abuse

Figure 6.5 Female Substance-Abuse
Offenders in U.S. Jails, in Percentages

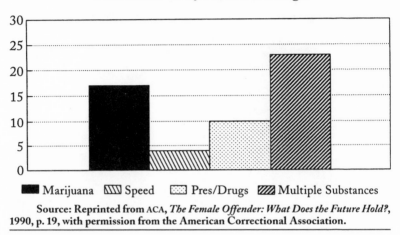

■ Marijuana ﬔ Speed   ▨ Pres/Drugs ▨ Multiple Substances

Source: Reprinted from ACA, *The Female Offender: What Does the Future Hold?*,
1990, p. 19, with permission from the American Correctional Association.

of substances in the African American community, revealed the following statistics:

1. Almost 8 million (36 percent of) blacks have used marijuana,
cocaine, or illicit drugs at least once in their lifetime;
2. Black women are more likely than women of any other racial
or ethnic group to have used crack cocaine; and
3. Black patients accounted for 39 percent (63,002) of the 160,170
drug abuse–related emergency room visits, and for 30 percent (1,999)
of the 6,756 drug abuse–related deaths reported by medical examin-
ers, which included 41 percent of the cocaine-related deaths and 31
percent of the heroin- or morphine-related deaths.

Along with these drug-abuse problems, female inmates also have
other disabilities that require equal attention. These disabilities are
shown in Figure 6.6.
The disabilities of female inmates are concentrated in two very
disturbing categories: learning disabled and emotionally disturbed.
Less common are visual, speech or hearing disabilities, a combination
of disabilities, and severe mental retardation.
Correctional institutions must provide trained personnel to deal

Figure 6.6 Disabilities of Female Inmates

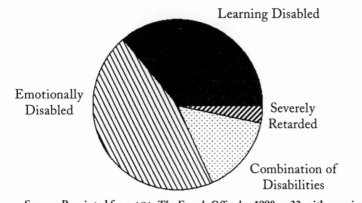

Learning Disabled

Emotionally Disabled

Severely Retarded

Combination of Disabilities

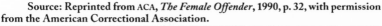

Source: Reprinted from ACA, *The Female Offender*, 1990, p. 32, with permission from the American Correctional Association.

with learning disabled, emotionally disturbed, and mentally retarded female inmates, as well as those with other disabilities.

Many African American women enter the prison system with multiple health problems. The majority of these problems are due in part to social factors (such as poverty) and the lack of access to comprehensive and coordinated medical services. As they enter the various levels of prison bureaucracy, prison health-care providers are now required to solve the health problems brought on by the social ills of U.S. society. The Eighth Amendment to the U.S. Constitution, which prohibits "cruel and unusual punishments," requires that all prisoners be provided with humane treatment.

When the prison health professionals are faced with the problems of substance abuse—particularly the consequences of alcohol and stimulant abuse, including poor nutrition, mental illness, poor prenatal care, sexually transmitted diseases, and now the AIDS virus—this already burdened prison system (due to overcrowding) simply cannot manage. Is it reasonable to expect the prison system to address these health conditions with the same level of quality health care available to the general public? What we can expect is exactly what has been the practice of most prison systems: the AIDS approach, which is crisis care, with no prevention, and very little if any health education. Therefore, these often sick African American women enter the prison system in poor health and most will leave with little noticeable change in their health status.

Chapter 7

Alternatives
to Incarceration

U.S. correctional administrators and criminal justice officials have continued to debate and reevaluate the purpose of incarceration. Some believe that the prison environment creates criminal personalities and helps to perpetrate further criminal behavior. Others feel that prisons are a necessary institution, needed to protect society and punish the offenders. Since we do not have a consensus as to what both benefits the female prisoners and at the same time protects society, our prison system should focus some of its attention on programs that rehabilitate women, while at the same time protecting society.

With more attention being given to women prisoners by civil and human rights organizations, national prison projects, and associations for female offenders, the public is becoming more aware of and sensitized to the prison officials' failure to rehabilitate thousands of African American women. Further, more attention and questioning has surfaced as to why those who commit nonviolent crimes should be incarcerated in prisons away from family and children for excessive, unfair lengths of time. With rising incarceration costs, partly fueled by increases in union-negotiated contracts and prison construction costs, some prison officials are looking to alternatives to lengthy incarcerations of women. In addition, women have a lower recidivism rate than men (other than for drugs), and in most cases are not career criminals. Therefore, rehabilitation efforts might prove to be of benefit to the inmate and society.

As Figure 7.1 shows, the majority of African American female inmates in federal prisons in 1990 had committed poverty crimes (for example, relating to property or drugs).

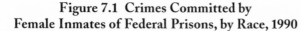

Figure 7.1 Crimes Committed by
Female Inmates of Federal Prisons, by Race, 1990

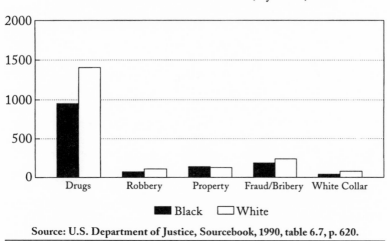

Source: U.S. Department of Justice, Sourcebook, 1990, table 6.7, p. 620.

Although the number of women inmates, in comparison to the number of males, is minuscule, there are an enormous number of African American women who are living behind prison walls. As explained in previous chapters, the court system, through biased sentencing practices and some male sexist judges, is more willing to send black women to prison without consideration of alternative programs like probation, weekend jail, halfway houses, therapeutic community centers, house arrest, and electronic monitoring. These options, if utilized, could drastically reduce the burden on already strained prison resources. In this chapter house arrest, electronic monitoring, and innovative residence programs will be highlighted.

House arrest programs, coupled with electronic monitoring, have surfaced as a cost-effective alternative to prison incarceration. The actual number of women prisoners who are afforded this option is not available. However, house arrest and electronic monitoring have a potential to benefit women by providing them with the opportunity to stay at home with their children and family while, at the same time, paying their debt to society.

In the house arrest program an inmate is confined to her home and her whereabouts are monitored by sophisticated technology. A form of this electronic monitoring telemetry system has been used extensively by hospitals to monitor patients with heart conditions.

Under this monitoring system, inmates who are confined to their homes can be monitored continuously by a signal that is sent to a monitoring station; or, an inmate can be periodically telephoned at specific times to see if she is at a particular location. The use of both types of equipment—telemetry and telephone—could serve as very useful programs for the courts.

A system that continuously monitors the whereabouts of an offender is available through a transmitter that is attached to the ankle. This type of device can effectively track an offender's movement inside a home and within a specific radius of the living quarters. The programmed type of devices, where the inmates are allowed to leave the home for work, doctor appointments, and even to pick up the children at the school bus stop, if used appropriately, could allow for substantial savings in foster care and correctional services. The computer that would be used in these situations can be programmed to telephone the offender at certain time intervals. There is voice verification technology that makes this kind of monitoring reliable.

The monitoring of this new type of prisoner has tripled annually since 1985 (*The* [Albany, N.Y.] *Sunday Gazette*, February, 17, 1991, p. B9). It was further reported that in 1990 there were over 12,000 people electronically monitored in the United States. The *Journal of Offender Monitoring* estimated that in 1991 there were between 25,000 to 50,000 people monitored in 47 states.

New York State continues to have one of the nation's largest female inmate populations. In 1990, of the 130,000 adults on probation, 500–600 were electronically monitored. However, data regarding how many African American women are afforded this opportunity is unavailable. It appears that those who are benefiting from the program are mainly white males.

In New York State, where it costs $80 million to build and $30 million to operate a prison annually, expanded electronic monitoring for female inmates could be a tremendous cost savings to New York residents.

Women for Human Rights and Dignity

There are also other types of noninstitutional sanctions that can be employed by the courts. Those who commit crimes must be punished for the crime. The courts must determine the appropriate sentence and the location of incarceration. When the judge makes the decision to incarcerate he or she must have available a set of options. Whether to send a female far away from her home to a prison in a rural community where it is difficult to see her family or participate in rehabilitative community services is usually determined by white male judges. One of those sanctions offered to women in New York State is located in this author's hometown of Buffalo, New York: the Women's Residential Resource Center, established in 1985. The impetus behind the establishment of the residence was the murder and mutilation of four children by an African American nursing student in her inner-city upstairs apartment.

The community was outraged when this woman, who was obviously mentally ill, was sentenced to life imprisonment in Bedford Hills Correctional Facility, located in New York State, rather than a psychiatric center. After spending a decade in prison, she was found not responsible by reason of insanity in the slaying of her son and three daughters, and is now sentenced to a guarded state psychiatric unit. The community was incensed that the courts in 1975 did not recognize that this mother was mentally ill and confine her at that time to a psychiatric center. Out of this injustice and tragedy a group of women founded Women for Human Rights and Dignity (WHRD).

The Women's Residential Resource Center was established under the leadership of Constance Eve, the wife of a New York State assemblyman. The residence began with a small staff for 10 residents who had been sentenced by the courts to 2 to 12 months of confinement.

The residence that accepts these offenders is a white Victorian, three-story home with turrets, leaded glass, crystal chandeliers, potted flowers, and a baby grand piano that graciously furnishes the elegant living quarters. The residence, which resembles a sorority house, has rules. All female residents must go to work, school, or social activities, wear their own clothing, clean their rooms, cook, and do their own laundry. The living quarters provide a homelike atmosphere, while improving the residents' self-esteem. Sometimes these options are not enough for the residents' survival, and they do abscond. For those who have difficulty adjusting to this environment, there are either disciplinary actions or a return to the courts for placement in the traditional correctional or prison facility.

The Women's Residential Resource Center's program not only provides a comfortable living environment, but has grown into a multiservice center with multiple programs that offer services and educational opportunities, preparing offenders to return to their family and community.

In 1989 the Women for Human Rights and Dignity established the Center for Educational and Vocational Enrichment where the offenders-residents of the Residential Resource Center could receive their high school equivalency diploma and certificates in various training programs which lead to economic independence. The WHRD continued to expand their program, and in 1991 established the One-Stop Center for Women. This center provides an expanded service that combines education and skilled training services in creative arts and workshops, along with meeting and planning space for residents. Some of the workshops concern family planning, self-conception, tough love, learning library skills, reading, job opportunities, legal issues for women, and exploring a holistic nursing approach.

The WHRD programming still gets better. In 1992 Dignity Circle was established to provide beautiful homes for families of former residents. In addition, since 1980 this same dedicated group of women and other volunteers has provided Christmas gifts for hundreds of children of incarcerated females in upstate New York correctional facilities. This project is appropriately titled Project Joy.

How do the residents feel about this wonderful program? The following is a reprint of one resident's feelings about it. Her remarks, along with those of other residents, are captured in a brochure printed by WHRD, featuring a collection of their stories and poems.

My Story
by a Resident of WHRD

Here at the Center for Educational and Vocational Enrichment and the Women's Residential Resource Center, I have learned many things and I will continue to learn as long as I stay with the program.

First of all, through Women for Human Rights and Dignity, Inc., and at the Women's Residential Resource Center, I am getting a few of the most important pieces of my life back, the parts that have pride and dignity attached to it. And believe it or not I am living proof that a 16-year-old, whether male or female can lose those things even though we as teenagers are just now receiving them. It is so hard to be an adolescent out here in the "real world." Especially when you are not there by choice. I guess that is why I consider myself lucky to have been chosen out of a few girls down at Delaware Avenue, also known as the Holding Center, to come to such a place as the Women's Residential Resource Center. And I am even more so privileged to be involved here along with my regular schooling at South Park High School. I receive the necessary education to acquire my high school diploma. In addition to that, I am learning to type and work with my hands in ceramic classes, both of which are things I enjoy doing.

I guess I could say that, of course, if I could do it all over again, a lot of things would be done differently. But since I, nor anyone I know, can turn back the clock, I am very thankful and also grateful to the Board, staff, other residents, and to the founder of this wonderful organization, Mrs. Constance B. Eve, for making my stay here both educational and enjoyable.

In conclusion, along with my other plans of becoming a criminal lawyer, I would like to come back one day to work along side Mrs. Eve as a volunteer in this wonderful environment that, for now, I call home.

I would like to take this opportunity to commend the women who have helped to make WHRD such a success.

Constance B. Eve, Chairperson

Betsy M. Strother	Louise Teamer Jackson
Hortense B. Nash	Peggy F. Johnson
Garnet H. Wallace	Judith M. Jones
Carolyn C. Balowitz	Nellie B. King
Thelma C. Batts	Muriel Moore
Pauline D. Childers	Mary Ruth Morrow
Gwendolyn Calhoun	Rev. K. Lwebuga-Mukasa
Erma Dean Robinson	Katherine M. Robinson
Geneva B. Scruggs*	Lisa M. Yaeger
Fern E. Beavers	

*Deceased.

From previous chapters, it is obvious that the judicial system is failing our African American women inmates, but we still incarcerate them in obsolete and unproductive systems of punishment. No one will disagree that society must be protected from dangerous criminals; but there are a number of programs, like those discussed, that are cost effective, rehabilitative, and protect the public.

Chapter 8

The Crime Bill:
Its Intent and Impact on
the African American Female

Americans have become obsessed with crime. This concern over-shadows all federal efforts to pass a national health policy. During the 1960s, the federal government funding of local and state law enforcement was the first real concerted effort to control crime. By the late 1980s we saw federal intervention shift to the war on drugs, which continues into the 1990s, despite losing battle after battle. For some communities it takes more than "Just say no."

An angry U.S. public—continuously fueled by television news, court TV, and newspaper editorials that daily keep before us shootings, stabbings, teen (boys and girls) gangs, the Olympic bombing in Atlanta, the World Trade Center bombing in New York, Susan Smith's drowning of her two children in Union, South Carolina, and the celebrated O.J. Simpson case—is scared and demanding relief. Furthermore, statistics verify the state of crime with "approximately 6.6 million violent crimes occurring in both 1981 and 1992" (*Congressional Digest*, June-July 1994, p. 167). In addition, the December 1994 Crime Clock released by the FBI ticks away as Americans commit crimes as follows:

1. One violent crime every 16 seconds;
2. One property crime every 3 seconds;
3. One murder every 12 minutes;
4. One robbery every 48 seconds; and
5. One burglary every 11 seconds.

The crime clock represents the annual ratio of crime to fixed time intervals (U.S. Department of Justice, Crime Clock-Release Sunday, 1994, p. 4). The federal government now sees itself even more involved than in the 1960s or 1980s.

Crime is big business, generating millions of jobs and prison construction contracts. With relentless media attention given to crime, Americans have summoned their legislative representatives for help. These legislative leaders started the debate and this culminated with President Clinton leading the charge. The end result of the debate was the Violent Crime Control and Law Enforcement Act of 1994 or, as it is better known, the Crime Bill.

When you examine each of the provisions, in the context of a biased criminal justice system, there are certain aspects of the bill that will have a devastating impact on the African American community and its African American female. As I reviewed the Violent Crime Control Law Enforcement Act of 1994 it occurred to me that it was a perfect example of how preoccupied Americans are with crime, and not with crime prevention.

In this chapter I will explore opposing views—pros and cons regarding the Crime Bill—and specifically Title II, prisons; Title III, crime prevention; Title IV, violence against women; and Title VI, death-penalty sections of the law, which will severely impact on the African American community in general and the African American female in particular.

Death Penalty: Impact on the African American Community

Under the federal drug "kingpin" death-penalty provision, 75 percent of those convicted were white and 25 percent were black, yet 78 percent of those selected for the death penalty were black while only 11 percent were white. This is but one of many glaring racial discrepancies that exist in the application of criminal penalties. Why has there been such a resurgence of the need to execute prisoners? One might wonder whether this has been the government's creative method and answer to reduce or control prison population; or one might wonder whether this new federal death-penalty law is similar to the Pig Law that followed the Civil War, where thousands of newly freed, hungry slaves who stole a pig would be sentenced to life on a prison plantation. This was state governments' way of legally condemning freed slaves back into slavery. Some people even feel that the death penalty is to be viewed as the governmental solution to reduce the number of African Americans (legalized genocide). Whatever we choose to believe, it is obvious that something is wrong.

Racial disparity in the sentencing process was documented in a February 1990 study by the Government Accounting Office. This report found that:

> in 82 percent of the studies, race of victims was found to influence the likelihood of being charged with capital murder or receiving the death penalty, i.e., those who murdered whites were found to be more likely to be sentenced to death than those who murdered blacks. This finding was remarkably consistent across data sets, states, data collection methods and analytic techniques [p. 5].

Further, this report shows that "more than half of the studies found that race of the defendant influenced the likelihood of being charged with a capital crime or receiving the death penalty." And it reported that "in one study, research found that in rural areas black defendants were more likely to receive death sentences" (p. 6).

As Barbara Rose Collins points out, "the United States locks up more people per capita than any other country. A whopping 25 percent of young black men are tangled up in the criminal justice system" (*Congressional Digest*, June-July 1994, p. 175). It is apparent that great caution and consideration had to be given by concerned legislators to such an important piece of legislation, knowing that prior to its passage there were only two federal death-penalty provisions. With the passage of the Crime Bill there would be a large number of new death-penalty crimes added to the current legislation. As the media continue to discuss and show violent crimes, Congress felt that the Crime Bill's death penalties would lead to less crime.

As previously mentioned, between 1930 and 1989 there were 33 women executed: 21 white and 12 black (U.S. Department of Justice, Office of Justice Programs, Bureau of Justice Statistics, Sourcebook 1990). These numbers, however, have escalated disproportionately since 1988, for 33 of the 37 federal death-penalty defendants have been African American. As reported in Charles Owen and Jimmy Bell's *Blacks and Criminal Justice* (1977), out of 3,859 legal executions in the United States, 53 percent were black, and some of the crimes for which blacks were sentenced to death are, at best, of questionable interpretation (p. 12).

While some have merely questioned the motives behind the Crime Bill, others have attempted to install some safeguards against the discriminatory way that the death penalty has been used against minorities. One such safeguard was the Racial Justice Act. This act was to allow courts to "consider evidence showing a consistent pattern of racially discriminatory death sentences in the sentencing jurisdiction, taking into consideration the nature of the cases being compared, the prior records of the offenders, and other statutorily appropriate nonracial characteristics" (*Congressional Digest*, June-July 1994, p. 170). Those who opposed the Racial Justice Act argued that it would be difficult to enforce the death penalty. Legislators felt that thousands of death-row inmates would challenge their sentence based on racial bias. Who were these lawmakers? African Americans have looked to Bill Clinton to be the president who cared. During his campaign, he expressed the notion of fair play. In fact, of his original cabinet members, six were white males, while blacks and Hispanics, 20 percent of the U.S. population, made up 43 percent of Clinton's cabinet. Therefore, African Americans felt that they had a voice in government. African Americans have traditionally voted Democratic because Democrats have always been viewed as the party that helps African Americans. However, when the Racial Justice Act was put before the legislative body for voting it was "the House, 211 Democrats, but only 5 Republicans, who voted against drafting the so-called Racial Justice Act, a provision in the Crime Bill that would have effectively eliminated capital punishment in any state in which a higher proportion of blacks than whites received the death penalty" (*USA Today*, November 16, 1994, p. 13A). Nevertheless, due to the "pork" that some legislators felt was contained in the Crime Bill, thus placing its passage in jeopardy, the president and the Democrats had to sacrifice the Racial Justice Act.

If the lawmakers of our nation would have included the Racial Justice Act in the Crime Bill it would have helped to not only safeguard the African American women who are on death row but also bring some credibility to the Crime Bill's questionable intent. Under the Federal Death Penalty Act of the Crime Bill there were nearly 60 new eligible crimes for the death penalty, according to the analysis of the American Civil Liberties Union (ACLU) in Washington, D.C. Their analysis divided the death-penalty provisions into three categories: (I) those that restore the death penalty for legislation held to be unconstitutional by the Furman Decision; (II) those that amend existing federal law to now provide for the death penalty; and (III) those that create new federal offenses and render them death-penalty eligible.

   I. Restoration of death penalty–eligible crimes that were rendered unconstitutional by the Furman Decision.* The following death-eligible crimes were reinstated:
      1. Air piracy resulting in death (49 U.S.C. and 1473);
      2. Bank robbery during the commission of which a killing occurs (18 U.S.C. and 2113(e));
      3. Destruction of aircraft or motor vehicle resulting in death (18 U.S.C. and 34);
      4. Espionage (18 U.S.C. and 793);
      5. First-degree murder (18 U.S.C. and 1111);
      6. First-degree murder of a foreign official or guest (18 U.S.C. and 1116);
      7. Kidnapping resulting in death (18 U.S.C. and 1201);
      8. Mailing of nonmailable items resulting in death (18 U.S.C. and 1716);
      9. Train-wrecking resulting in death (18 U.S.C. and 1992);
      10. Treason (18 U.S.C. and 2381); and
      11. Use of explosive materials resulting in death (18 U.S.C. and 844(d)).
  II. Expansion of existing crimes to death penalty–eligible offenses:
      1. Being a principal organizer of a multimillion-dollar drug ring (18 U.S.C. and 3591(b)(1));
      2. Carjacking resulting in death (18 U.S.C. and 2119);
      3. Deprivation of civil rights resulting in death (18 U.S.C. and 241, 242, 245, 247);
      4. Genocide (18 U.S.C. and 1091);
      5. Hostage taking where death results (18 U.S.C. and 1203);
      6. Interstate travel or use of interstate facilities in connection with murder for hire (18 U.S.C. and 1958);
      7. Murder in aid of racketeering (18 U.S.C. and 1959);
      8. Sexual abuse resulting in death (18 U.S.C. and 2245); and
      9. Trafficking in large quantities of drugs (18 U.S.C. and 3591(b)(1)).

*Reinstates the death penalty for all the federal statutes held to be unconstitutional by the Supreme Court decision in Furman. This legislation lay dormant for over 20 years following the Furman decision.

III. New federal offenses were created that rendered the death penalty eligible:
  1. Alien smuggling that results in death (18 U.S.C. and 1324(a)(1)(B)(iv));
  2. Attempted homicide in a federal facility; (18 U.S.C. and 930(c));
  3. Attempting to kill a public officer, juror, witness, or family member of an officer, juror, or witness in order to obstruct the investigation or prosecution of a continuing criminal enterprise (18 U.S.C. and 3591(b)(2));
  4. Drive-by shooting in furtherance of drug conspiracy that results in death (18 U.S.C. and 36);
  5. First-degree murder of a United States national abroad (18 U.S.C. and 1118);
  6. Gun murder during a crime of violence (18 U.S.C. and 924(i));
  7. Gun murder during an attack on a federal facility (18 U.S.C. and 930(c));
  8. Homicide during an attack on a federal facility (18 U.S.C. and 930(c));
  9. Intentional infliction of serious bodily injury that results in death (18 U.S.C. and 359(a)(2)(B));
  10. Intentional killing (18 U.S.C. and 359(a)(2)(A));
  11. Intentional killing of a state or local officer, an official working with federal law enforcement officers, or a state correctional officer by a federal prisoner or in the course of interstate transport of a federal prisoner (18 U.S.C. and 1121);*
  12. Intentionally participating in an act of violence that constitutes a reckless disregard for human life, where the victim dies as a direct result of the act (18 U.S.C. and 359(a)(2)(D));
  13. Killing court officers or jurors (18 U.S.C. and 1503(b));
  14. Killing witnesses, victims, or informants with the intent to retaliate (18 U.S.C. and 1513(a));

This provision alone contains 8 different offenses. First, the killing can be done either at a federal prison or during interstate transport of a federal prisoner; and second, there are 4 different victims that can trigger this provision. Four victims with 2 different killing locations means that 8 different crimes are contained within this 1 provision.

15. Knowingly directing, advising, authorizing or assisting another in the attempt to kill a public officer, juror, witness, or family member of an officer, juror, or witness in order to obstruct the investigation or prosecution of a continuing criminal enterprise (18 U.S.C. and 3591(b)(2));*
16. Murder by an escaped federal prisoner (18 U.S.C. and 1120);
17. Murder by a federal life-term prisoner (18 U.S.C. and 1119);
18. Murder of a U.S. national during a terrorist act outside the United States (18 U.S.C. and 2332(a)(1));
19. Murder of a federal law enforcement official (18 U.S.C. and 1114);
20. Murder of a U.S. national by a terrorist outside the United States (18 U.S.C. and 2332);
21. Sexual exploitation resulting in death (18 U.S.C. and 2251(d));
22. Torture that leads to death (18 U.S.C. and 2340(a));
23. Using a weapon of mass destruction that results in death (18 U.S.C. and 2332(a));
24. Violence against maritime navigation in which death results (18 U.S.C. and 2280);
25. Violence against a fixed platform in which death results (18 U.S.C. and 2281);
26. Violence against a facility or aircraft at an international airport that results in death (18 U.S.C. and 37); and
27. Violence against a person at an international airport that results in death (18 U.S.C. and 37).

The ACLU also noted that as of July 1994, there were 2,870 people on state death rows. By June 1996 there were 3,000 people on death row, with 56 executions in 1995 (*NBC Nightly News*, June 5, 1996).

Under the Crime Bill, the federal death penalty will not be carried out while a woman is pregnant. In addition, if a woman is mentally retarded and lacks the capacity to understand why it was imposed she will not be put to death.

Combined with the attempt crimes, 18 U.S.C. and 3591(b)(2) alone contains over 10 death-eligible permutations. There are 4 possible victims. Additionally, there are at least 3 degrees of participation: attempting to kill, authorizing an attempt to kill, or assisting in an attempt to kill. This means that there are at least 12 crimes within just 1 provision of the F.D.P.A.

Table 8.1 Female Violent Crimes, State Prisons, 1986

	White	*Black*
Homicide	51.2	46.0
Murder	36.0	27.2
Manslaughter	15.5	19.0

Source: U.S. Department of Justice, Sourcebook 1990, p. 620.

How Will "Three Strikes and You're Out" Affect the African American Community?

A criminal justice system that is far from being color blind in its sentencing practices will have plenty of legal muscle when it applies Title VII, which provides for mandatory life imprisonment for persons convicted of certain felonies: "Three Strikes and You're Out."

In the United States, where 50 to 60 percent of all crimes are committed by persons between 10 and 20 years of age and the incidence of crime peaks between the ages of 16 and 18, this law will send many young women to prison. In a system that is already biased against women, this section of the bill can be devastating for women who are addicted to controlled substances. Data in Chapter 6 documents the number of African American females who are convicted and sentenced for drug-abuse offenses and sent to prison. The law states that

> a person who is convicted in a court of the United States of a serious violent felony shall be sentenced to life imprisonment if the person has been convicted (and the conviction has been finalized) on separate prior occasions in a court in the United States or of a state; two or more serious felonies; or one or more serious violent felonies and one or more serious drug offenses [HR 3355 Crime Bill, pp. 217–18].

Some of the areas that the law denotes as "serious felonies" are firearms use, manslaughter, and assault with intent to commit murder. Although men still outrank women in the number of serious felonies (for example, murder), females are committing an increasing number of violent crimes, as is presented in Table 8.1.

According to Table 8.1, white women outranked African American women in all categories except manslaughter. Then why are African American women overrepresented in the state prison population?

Clearly, we do not have the details of the crimes that all the women have committed, but we certainly need to ask why this is so.

What's more, the American Correctional Association (1990) reported that substance abuse among females (43.4 percent white and 36 percent black) at the time of intake in state prison was as follows: marijuana, 46 percent; cocaine, 27 percent; crack, 16 percent; and heroin, 14 percent. Substance abuse among federal female inmates indicated that 66 percent of white women and 63.4 percent of black women were confined for drug-abuse offenses.

How the law will be applied is of grave concern where there appear to be rewards (that is, Crime Bill state grants) for imposing stringent sentencing.

Building Walls

Blacks are more exploitable because they are the subjugated minority. One of the major factors is the discretion that police officers have on whether to arrest or not. These police officers' decisions, unlike judges who are controlled to some extent by statute, make it a very difficult situation to control (see Chapter 9 below). With this in mind, the prison cells will be constructed and filled, in most instances, with poor women of color. Under Title II of the Crime Bill, there are substantial funds (grants) to assist local and state agencies with the construction of new prison cells. To be eligible for grant funding, local communities must demonstrate that they are pursuing and sentencing offenders who will serve a substantial portion of the sentence imposed. Since black women are overrepresented in the prison system, this law can then be used to their disadvantage by states like Ohio, whose prisons are at 182 percent capacity (*Congressional Digest*, June-July 1994, p. 178) to help ease their overcrowded cells. Prior to the passage of the Crime Bill, prison expansion was under way with the Bureau of Prison budget, which had planned for the opening of six new facilities in May 1991; 13 new prisons in 1992; and 14 in 1994 and 1995; for a total of 47 new facilities (not including 16 prison expansions, 1992–94). The Crime Bill made prison expansion and construction attractive to state officials, since they have been grappling with a 115.3 percent increase over nine years (1980–89) in the federal and state inmate population. This expansion and construction also pleases state prison officials because it allows for boot camps and some community services. Nevertheless, "if the war against crime is to be won, it will be won not in the cellblocks of our prisons, but in the schools, churches, playgrounds, work places and homes within the community" (Biles, 1988, p. 55).

Ounce of Prevention: Help for Communities

Under Title III, crime prevention communities can request funds to support a variety of community-based programs. The Crime Bill provides for block and discretionary grants.

About 2 billion dollars is designated for state and local governments to be distributed under the block grants' guidelines. These grants are calculated on that community's crime rate, taxes, unemployment, and population. The funding of the Crime Bill and the preventions programs are funded from a Violent Crime Reduction Trust Fund. This trust fund receives money for six years from the federal government by the redirecting of salaries of retiring employees whose positions are eliminated. It is estimated that the fund will get as much as $800 million over a six-year period. This would at least provide the funds for prevention programs, unless the two houses of Congress change the provisions (see below). This is the danger of such laws that can be defunded, yet the "Three Strikes and You're Out" and the death-penalty provisions remain intact. What is unique about the funding is that communities can apply directly to Washington (for example, to the Department of Justice) and the vice president will chair an Ounce of Prevention Council.

Some of the programs that will impact on African American women are discussed below.

Violence against women—the apparent self-destructive behavior among residents of the African American community—has brought media attention. Many articles and newscasts feature nightly stories of black on black crimes (Flowers, 1990). In 1994 roughly 17.3 percent more black women died as a result of accidents than did white women (p. 85). And more recently, the Center for Mental Health Services conference on the abuse of women reported the following alarming statistics:

1. Each day in the United States 10 women die as a result of domestic violence;

2. Every 15 seconds a woman is beaten;

3. Every 6 minutes a woman is raped; and

4. 45 percent of mothers who abuse their children were abused themselves.

The victimization of black women started when they were first brought to this country and forced into slavery. First victimized by American whites who exploited their abilities to work, they were forced to work long hours on the master's plantation; then their reproductive ability meant they were forced at a young age to bear large numbers of children; and lastly, their sexuality was exploited in the master's bedroom. This exploitation continues in the United States in many ways today. Black women continue to be arrested, convicted, and sent to prison for crimes more often than their white counterparts, who are often sent home to their families. Flowers (1990) reported that black women are eight times more likely to be imprisoned than white females and face at least a six times greater likelihood of imprisonment than other minority groups of females (p. 86). The African slave woman was the first minority female brought to this nation to work, preceding other ethnic minority females, yet they still are treated with more abuse, neglect, and exploitation than the women who followed. This exploitation is further perpetuated within their own community by their own black men, especially men who exploit their sexuality by selling the women into a life of prostitution. What leads the black woman into a life as a streetwalker? Jennifer James (1977) noted three categories that have the potential to motivate women to become streetwalkers and prostitutes.

1. Conscious: Economic, working conditions, adventure, a persuasive pimp;

2. Situational: Early experiences in life, parental abuse and/or neglect, an occupation; and

3. Psychoanalytic: General factors, Oedipal fixation, latent homosexuality, and retardation (p. 390).

African American women who are arrested for prostitution fall primarily into the Conscious category, because of their economic status: many of them live below the poverty level (32 percent in 1990), they are miseducated with no hopes of employment, and they have persuasive pimps who capitalize on the women's inability to support their children or drug habits. The Situational category is that where the woman has experienced parental abuse and neglect and is the category within which falls the highest number of inmates who have minimal skills and who are unemployed at the time of arrest. Supported by the Bureau of Justice Statistics Survey of State Prison Inmates in 1991— which notes that 4 in every 10 women reported that they had been abused at least once before their arrest—34 percent reported being physically abused, and 34 percent had been sexually abused before age 18 (p. 6). And for the Psychoanalytic category, as presented in Chapter 3, there are large numbers of mentally retarded women incarcerated in state facilities. James's findings were criticized because they were not considered representative of all situations (Flowers, 1987). However, "there are no pretty women" as in the motion picture that depicts a beautiful white prostitute who makes $1,000 a trick and falls in love with a wealthy john, who sweeps her away in his stretch limousine. In the black community there are no such prostitutes. Instead there are streetwalker women who hide in dark corners waiting to turn a trick for $5, risking AIDS, assault, and even death because of their encounters. These black female streetwalkers are the ones who have the highest arrest rate because of their exposure on the street curbs. They are not the call girls who live on Madison Avenue and have a Mayflower Madam to serve as the pimp. These are usually white upper class women with stable, drug-free lives and who are seldom arrested because they are protected by the high-powered attorneys hired by the Madam. These women, however, are equally exploited and victimized.

Violence Against Women

The Violence Against Women Act contains $1.6 billion in funding beginning in the fiscal year 1995. This act is designed to protect women and prosecute those who harm them. Under the federal penalties for sex crimes, repeat offenders who sexually abuse are "punishable by a term of imprisonment up to twice that otherwise authorized" (HR 3355, p. 137). This section of the law also allows for a victim of sexual abuse to receive restitution for the crime. The court system is required to set up a mechanism for the victim to receive the full amount of loss she has incurred (for example, medical or psychiatric care and wages). There are also grants for communities to combat and reduce violent crimes against women. These grants can also be used to combat domestic violence by training law enforcement officers about the need to enforce orders of protection. It also supports grants that would focus on ethnic minorities (black) to help provide domestic violence court advocates.

The overrepresentation of minority women in the prison system— perpetuated by a court system that has been shown (see Chapter 2) to be biased when prosecuting and sentencing African American females—is the target of section 40421 of the Crime Bill. Under this section, "to gain a better understanding of the nature and the extent of gender bias in federal courts, the circuit's judicial councils are encouraged to conduct studies of the instance, if any, of gender bias in their respective circuits and to implement recommended reforms" (p. 179). It was suggested that gender study should not only examine judges but also should include witnesses, attorneys, and jurors. The training the judges received hopefully will help them if their local government agrees to participate and submits a grant for funding under Title V, drug court. This section of the Crime Bill allows for local courts to supervise non-violent offenders who have substance-abuse problems. A judge could require periodic testing of those addicted and on supervised release or probation. As presented in Chapter 3, African American women are more likely to use crack cocaine (the cheap high) more often than white or Hispanic women. With a program that is geared toward an alternative to prison, yet has some offender management, health care, and education services, it is instituted by a judge and court system that has been sensitized to their needs and so could be of great benefit to them. Drug court will begin its 1995 fiscal year with a $1 billion allocation.

African American woman are subjected to cruel punishment by the drug pushers, pimps, and the courts. They are often without the resources to escape this torture or their community lacks the appropriate resources to assist them. Under the Safe Homes for Women Act, another section of the Crime Bill (p. 159), a national domestic violence hotline will be established. This toll-free telephone line will provide referral services and counseling on a 24-hour basis. Much needed shelter information throughout the United States will help these woman to leave an abusive situation and start anew. There are also severe penalties for a person who travels across a state line with the intent to injure, harass, or intimidate their spouse (HR 3344, p. 161). And once again, an attempt is made to educate judges in criminal and other courts about domestic violence to help improve their disposal of such cases (HR 3344, p. 167).

One of the most important aspects of the law that has far-reaching implications on the overrepresentation of African Americans in prison is the Equal Justice for Women in Court Act. The act provides training for judges and court personnel in laws dealing in domestic and other crimes of violence that are motivated by the victim's gender.

Training for judges is extremely important when African American women are involved. When these women come before the courts they are usually before white males. In 1981 women made up 14 percent of the nation's lawyers and judges. Black men represented only 19 percent and black women only 0.8 percent of these positions (Staples, 1994, p. 245). As discussed by Rita Simon and Jean Landes, "judges often say that they cannot help but compare a woman defendant with other women whom they know well—namely, their mothers and wives—and others whom they cannot imagine behaving in the manner attributed to the defendant" (Simon and Landes, 1991, p. 57). Therefore, since these white male judges equate most of their experiences with white mothers and wives, they need to be sensitized to the plight of African American women and the crimes that bring them to the court systems. As previously mentioned in Chapter 2, some believe that women receive preferential treatment before the courts. This may be true as it relates to white women (see below), which may account for their low representation in the prisons throughout the United States, while their African American counterparts occupy most of America's female prison cells.

Numerous studies have confirmed the harsh treatment of black women in the U.S. courts. One study by Mary Owens of a Chicago woman's court appearance exemplifies their treatment, as reported in the book by Jeffrey Reiman. The findings are as follows:

> Judges found 16 percent of the white women brought before them on charges of shoplifting to be "not guilty," but only 4 percent of the black women were found innocent. In addition, 22 percent of the black women as compared to only 4 percent of the white women were sent to jail. Finally, of the 21 white women sent to jail only 2 (10%) were to be jailed for 30 days or more; of the 76 black women sentenced to jail, 20 (26%) were to be jailed for 30 days or more [Reiman, 1979, p. 117].

Others, like Christy Visher (1983) and Clarice Feinman (1986), have studied gender and race issues in the courts and have ascertained that there are differences. For example, Feinman states that "chivalry is reserved for white middle- and upper-class women, except those who deviate from culturally expected behavior for ladies" (p. 28); and Visher found that in encounters with police officers those female suspects who violated typical middle-class standards of traditional characteristics and behavior (such as those that white, older, and submissive persons would show) were not afforded any chivalrous treatment during arrest decisions. In these data, young, black, or hostile women received no preferential treatment, whereas older white women who were calm and deferential toward the police were granted leniency (p. 23).

Whatever motivates judges in today's court, the "I Remember Mama" attitude does not work for African American women. What the data tell us is that leniency and chivalry are dead when applied to African American females. The plight of women, specifically African Americans, in a biased court system is further discussed in Chapter 10.

As pointed out in this chapter, the Crime Bill has some qualities that will certainly impact favorably against the abuse of women: a national domestic-abuse hotline, more severe punishment of women batterers, restitution for crimes committed, and better drug treatment programs. However, the funding of these services is only as good as the resources allocated for their delivery. If the established trust fund is cut or eliminated, we will be left with laws and no prevention program funds. The 1994 election of a very conservative Congress is an indicator as to whether the few positive aspects of the Crime Bill will continue after the six-year funding limit. Their election serves as a reminder to a previously noted concern: Americans are more preoccupied with crime than they are with good health care.

The Crime Bill Revisited

With the takeover by Republicans of both houses of Congress, the 1994 Crime Bill was targeted for a revisit by very conservative lawmakers. As previously mentioned, the Crime Bill will adversely impact on African Americans. The Republicans considered the following changes to the 1994 Crime Bill: to transfer the proposed allocation for crime prevention to prison construction; to make it easier to apply the death penalty; and install new mandatory minimums.

Further, the House Judiciary Subcommittee during their Crime Law Revision hearing (C-SPAN, January 19, 1995) heard testimony from the criminal justice community that supported constraints on the filing of the writ of *habeas corpus* by prisoners.

Habeas corpus, Latin for "you should have the body," enables an inmate to challenge a criminal conviction, an administrative procedure, a prison regulation, or a condition of confinement that violates his or her rights under the Constitution (Jim Thomas, 1988, p. 75). Under this procedure, the inmate usually files a written statement that challenges the confinement. The judge then reviews the inmate complaint and renders a decision as to whether the imprisonment was lawful. Sometimes the inmate is released or a new trial is ordered.

California inmates file 1,100 lawsuits each year. A total of 56 full-time California attorneys deal specifically with prisoners' lawsuits, which cost this state $10 million each year (C-SPAN, January 19, 1995).

If *habeas corpus* and the right to appeal restrict the inmate from filing a complaint, the prisoners have no voice outside the prison walls, nor one who can objectively look at their situation. Women file the fewest writs of *habeas corpus*. However, as noted earlier, these prisoners are beginning to file more complaints.

Restrictions on appeals would have devastating effects in death-penalty cases. A 1992 study by James Leibman, a professor at Columbia University Law School, showed that 42 percent of *habeas corpus* petitions filed in state capital cases from 1976 to 1991 resulted in finding a reversible constitutional error; this was true in fewer than 5 percent of the cases involving noncapital crimes (*New York Times*, December 30, 1994). What is also of grave concern is that there are certain restrictions, under a U.S. Supreme Court ruling, that curtail the access of death row inmates to legal assistance where state or federal courts may have to hear issues not addressed in other appeals. The end result is that lawyers and legal firms are requested to volunteer their time and resources to investigate mistakes that the inmate's trial attorney may have made in her trial proceedings. Several New York State firms like Paul, Weiss, Rifkind, Wharton and Garrison; Skadden, Arps, Slate, Meagher and Flom; and Sullivan and Cromwell have represented death-row inmates (*New York Times*, December 30, 1994). According to the California state attorney general, there are 400 prisoners currently on death row in California. Figure 8.1 shows that this number continues to rise.

As Eleanor Jackson Peel, who is attempting to educate lawyers on capital appeals, states: "We have an obligation to the whole legal system to try to make it less unjust to the people who somehow don't matter" (*New York Times*, December 30, 1994).

In 1994 we witnessed a liberal president sign the Crime Bill, which was then left up to a conservative Congress to fund and implement.

The final Crime Bill, as the National Association for the

Figure 8.1
Head Count on Death Row

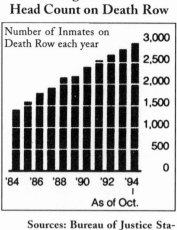

Number of Inmates on
Death Row each year

3,000
2,500
2,000
1,500
1,000
500
0

'84   '86   '88   '90   '92   '94

As of Oct.

Sources: Bureau of Justice Statistics ('84-'85); NAACP Legal Defense and Education Fund ('86-'94).

Advancement of Colored People (NAACP) stated in their August 2, 1994, letter to the House of Representatives, "is fundamentally flawed when examined in the light of the principle of equality under the law for all persons in the United States ... the further extension of ... the federal death penalty to over 50 new crimes. Yet, there is mounting evidence which strongly suggests that race plays a significant role in capital prosecutions and sentences." With this major concern, the NAACP urged lawmakers to include the Racial Justice Act as a safety net and antidiscrimination provision in the bill, but this was eliminated from the final version of the act. The elimination of the safety net, combined with a conservative-controlled Senate, the Republican-sponsored Contract with America, the revisit of the Crime Bill, as well as increased numbers of conservative state legislators, and 34 Republican governors, has escalated the fear of the subjective use of the death penalty when applied to blacks. Where education at an early age could help young African American children learn the skills of healthy living—the foundation of the Head Start program—these programs are scheduled to be reviewed and cut. And the Rev. Jesse Jackson, during an Operation Push meeting, stated that "instead of stressing the positive points, Democrats were intimidated by Republicans on crime issues, ... they tried to compete with Republicans by peddling fear" (*Buffalo News*, November 13, 1994, p. 8A). He further noted that where blacks had been promised more opportunities, even though the Clinton administration had created five million jobs, instead they got more jails in the Crime Bill. Although the Crime Bill has the overall potential to disproportionately impact adversely on African American women, there are some aspects that might help eliminate exploitation and domestic violence. In addition, the funding of training for judges and other court-appointed personnel hopefully will bring better understanding and fairness into the prosecution and sentencing of African American women. Finally, better drug treatment for prisoners and health care in general has the potential to impact recidivism.

Chapter 9

A Day in
a U.S. Court: The Endless
Parade of African Americans

I invite you to spend, as I did, a day in a U.S. courtroom, where African Americans are being incarcerated at an alarming rate. Is this incarceration legitimate or is it a form of underground racism, which Congressman Kweisi Mfume has labeled "subterranean racism"? In their criminology text, Edwin Southerland and Donald Cressey (1974) state that "Numerous studies have shown that African Americans are more likely to be arrested, indicted, convicted and committed to an institution than whites who commit the same offenses" (p. 133).

Has what is referenced in the above quotation changed in two decades? According to the U.S. General Accounting Office (February 1990), a synthesis of 28 studies showed "a pattern of evidence indicating racial disparity in the charging, sentencing and imposition of the death penalty" (p. 4).

Police officers who have almost unlimited discretion to arrest or not to arrest have the greatest impact on the criminal justice court system. The police officer, who is inundated at the police academy with arrest data that show the large number of African American women who have committed crimes, are arrested, and incarcerated, is thus in many cases preconditioned to believe that this particular population is more prone to crime. What is not known by these mainly white officers is the number of whites who may have been given a mere slap on the wrist and let go, or the number of white officers who may completely dismiss the possibility that a nice, white, suburban, young female (who looks like his sister or daughter) would ever commit such a crime.

Heaven forbid that such a person should be arrested and put into jail! Therefore, she escapes the arrest while her African American counterpart, who may have committed the same crime, gets arrested.

As the new Republican force behind Contract with America took shape, there was a renewed interest to revisit the 1994 Crime Bill, particularly the section that dealt with the police program. The 1994 Crime Bill supplied $8.8 billion over a six-year period for approximately 100,000 extra police nationwide. For 1995, $1.3 billion has been allocated for the police program. With more police officers—the vast majority of whom will be white males—will the arrest rate of African American women continue to escalate? A study by John Hepburn (1978) found that white officers were more willing to serve arrest warrants on nonwhite females (72 percent) as opposed to white females (54 percent). Also, as reported by Marshall Meyers (1980), blacks were more often fatally shot or shot at by Los Angeles police.

With the disproportional endless stream of African Americans in the U.S. courts, these studies help to validate what may be the underlying contributors to this disparity.

During my time in a U.S. criminal court (December 1994)* as an observer, I witnessed this endless march of African American city residents through the court system, almost exclusively accompanied by a public defender.

Of the 46 defendants, 38 were male (11 Hispanic, 22 black, 3 Chinese, 2 white) and 8 were female (7 black, 1 white). From this small sample, as suspected, males continued to outnumber female in arrests, but female defendants largely resembled male arrests in terms of race, ethnic background, and age. These women also closely mirrored the offenses for which women are sentenced to prison terms. As reported in the U.S. Department of Justice, Bureau of Justice Statistics, Survey of State Prison Inmates, 1991, "Women in Prison," major offenses were related to: violence, 32 percent; property, 28.7 percent; and drugs, 32.8 percent. From the above small sample there were three related to property, two to prostitution, two to drugs, and one to other charges. Following arrest and before imprisonment lies a very important process that will help to determine whether a female is innocent or guilty of a crime. As previously mentioned, black women who go before the courts

---

*The author acknowledges with thanks the opportunity to join two criminal court jurists on the bench in a large Northeast city court and is particularly appreciative of the chief judge and staff for their administrative assistance.

have the least chance of being adjudicated not guilty. There are several reasons why this appears to be so. First, one of the above-mentioned black female defendants, who happened to be the only one of the eight females represented by a privately retained counsel, was not well-served by her attorney. He openly argued in court with the female judge hearing the case because he wanted the court calendar for his black female client's reappearance to accommodate his trial schedule. The district attorney who wanted $500 for bail, of course, got it. Secondly, assigned counsel for *pro bono* cases usually are overworked and unable to devote the needed time to do the necessary preparation for an appropriate defense. Thirdly, there are legal aid or public defenders who are assigned incredible caseloads. They, too, are overworked and have little time for preparation, and so the defense may suffer. As a result, for most of the defendants—who are usually poor—bail is out of the question. Therefore, these women must sit in jail until the court calendar and public defender or *pro bono* attorney are ready to act. (Unless the judge releases them on their own recognizance, which, if they have a long arrest record, is a poor risk for a return date.) Thus, the punishment begins while they are really still legally innocent. In the cases of these black women, they are, in effect, guilty until their attorney can prepare a defense.

Once the attorney is ready to act, he and his client must face in some cases biased judges and juries. There have been numerous reports of attempts to uncover how judges decide on the punishments for those who come before the court. In one study, which focused on African American women, Mary Owens-Cameron studied the sentencing practices of Chicago's women's court judges (1964). She discovered that "Judges found 16 percent of white women brought before them on charges of shoplifting to be not guilty, but only 4 percent of black women were found innocent. In addition, 22 percent of the black women as compared to only 4 percent of the white women were sent to jail."

Within the decisions that judges make regarding fines, sentencing, bail, plea bargaining, and alternatives to incarceration there exists some flexibility that may or may not benefit the defendant. Because judges are human, they, too, must have human emotions. How emotions, attitudes, and thinking help to determine or influence a judge's decision on sentencing lengths for African American female defenders was the subject of a brief questionnaire.* The sample included

---

*In deference to the busy schedule of jurists, the questionnaire contained only four questions, one of which was optional.

approximately 75 county, state, city, and supreme court judges in both suburban and large urban areas. Twelve judges responded to the following questions:

1. Please list those female characteristics that help you to determine your sentence.

Response: Age, employment, physical conditions, disability, family background, education, IQ, marital status, nature of the offense, prior record, victims, and care and number of children.

2. Does race, culture, or education help you decide on sentencing?

Response: Education may be a factor, race and culture are not. Race, culture, and education are all factors.

As was previously quoted, "Judges often say that they cannot help but compare a woman defendant with other women whom they know well—namely, their mothers and wives—and others whom they cannot imagine behaving in the manner attributed to the defendant" (Simon and Landes, 1991, p. 57). I would assume that a majority of those judges referred to in the above citation are white males. This assumption is based on the following information. "In 1981 women made up 14 percent of the nation's lawyers and judges, up from 4 percent in 1971, while black men had gained only 1.9 percent and black women only 0.8 percent of these positions" (Staples, 1994, p. 245).

Further, in an article by Sheila Weller, it was noted that women are entering law schools in great numbers and the legal profession could be close to 40 percent female by the year 2000. This means that 25 percent of the nation's judges will be women in 20 years (Weller, 1992, p. 94). Would this really make a difference in how women defendants are treated? African American females who are sitting judges tend to bring to the bench experiences that many women have had. They have husbands, children, housework, and civic responsibilities. Also, they should be aware, through their own experiences, of how it feels to be discriminated against in most aspects of U.S. society. They should also bring with them the sensitivities of the African American community. This may not always be the case, as California U.S. Court of Appeals Judge Stephen Rhinhardt points out, "There are some women judges, however, who are to women what Clarence Thomas is to blacks. Selecting a judge from a particular group doesn't assure that a person will represent the view or sensitivities of that group. More women than men may have more sensitivity on certain issues, but not all women do" (Weller, 1992, p. 104).

With a dearth of studies that deal with African American female jurists, the following is by no means representative of all African American jurists but they are two brief examples of federal judiciary.

In *Hattin v. Ford Motor Company*, the black female judge ruled that the company had unlawfully discriminated against the plaintiff (Davis, 1989, p. 76). In Davis's analysis of this decision he noted that black male and female jurists were "similar in their approach in handling racial discrimination cases" (p. 76). He further noted in his review of decisions rendered that male and female black jurists, with a few exceptions, were essentially conservative arbiters, as is true for the vast majority of their white counterparts (p. 78).

Do black judges make a difference? This has been the subject of a number of articles: Welch, Combs, and Gruhl, 1988; David Smith, 1983; Crockett, 1984; and Spohn, 1990. In taking a look at these studies, Welch investigated whether black judges' sentencing of black offenders was different from that of white judges. Since African Americans are perceived as being more liberal and most belong to the Democratic Party, which is portrayed as the champion of the poor and the underprivileged, it was felt that some of these attitudes would seep through in their decisions when prosecuting black defendants. In the Susan Welch, Michael Combs, and John Gruhl (1988) study, the sample population (3,418 males) was drawn from a large metro city group of felony convictions that were decided by 10 black and 130 white judges. Regarding prison sentences, they "found that white judges are more likely to send black defendants to prison than they are white defendants ... black judges tend to sentence black and white defendants to prison at about the same rate" (p. 132).

The investigators felt that black judges might be attempting to be fair in their treatment of all defendants, whereas white judges were more severe with blacks and less severe with white defendants. With the white judges (130) outnumbering the African American judges (10), the impact of their decisions on African Americans are devastating. Further, in sentencing severity "black judges appear even handed, while white judges are less likely to send white defendants to prison" (p. 134). Cassia Spohn (1990) also compared the sentencing decisions of black and white jurists. Her findings render some disturbing information that could, if it were the norm, have further devastating effects on the incarceration of African Americans. This study found that "both black and white judges sentence black offenders more severely than white offenders" (p. 1197).

Not all African American jurists fall into these categories. One of the most controversial judges, Bruce Wright, who was labeled "Turn 'Em Loose Bruce," sought justice for those he saw as the most unjustly treated in the Manhattan Criminal Court system. Judge Wright, who freed many who could not make bail, felt that their rights under the Eighth Amendment to the U.S. Constitution were being violated by excessive bail demands. Further, in the 1970s, he came under fire by the police, who criticized him for releasing a man without bail who had been arrested for allegedly slashing a police officer's throat. Judge Wright does not fall into the previously cited categories. With the power that judges have to interpret the statutes, fix bail, convict, and sentence, Judge Wright used his authority to interpret the law (the Eighth Amendment) and, as he saw it, to apply it fairly. He served from 1982 in the New York State Supreme Court hearing civil cases, and retired in 1995 at the age of 76, still revered and held in high esteem by his community.

Judges are selected from many areas of society, and they come to the courts from various law schools, institutions that may have an impact on their thinking of how the law should be applied. However, if selected for a federal appointment, their colleagues have certainly chosen them with care. It is felt by some that the selection criteria for appointed black judges may be beneficial to black offenders, because they bring to the position sensitivity and knowledge of the concerns of the inner cities. On the other hand, if elected (to supreme or city courts) they must be affiliated with a political party to which they have paid their dues (sold tickets or made campaign contributions) and are therefore eligible for a nomination to fill vacated judgeships. The elective versus appointive process could hold the judge accountable by questioning his or her intentions prior to the election. But in municipalities where there is one dominant political party African American judicial candidates may or may not get the party nod.

The New York City court system in 1994 came under fire for violations of an order under the federal voting act.*

---

*Under the Voting Rights Act the state is supposed to obtain preapproval or preclearance from the Justice Department before instituting any election law changes that affect minority voters living in the boroughs of the Bronx, Brooklyn, and Manhattan (Wise, 1994, p. 1).

Apparently, it has been the practice that court of claims judges, who are appointed by the governor, are in turn appointed as acting state supreme court justices. These justices are then assigned to criminal court as a means of alleviating the backlog of cases. Unlike state supreme court justices, who are elected to serve for 14-year terms, acting justices do not run in any election (Goldstein, 1994, p. 1) for the seat to which they were appointed. Therefore, the seat may be held indefinitely.

Because of this situation, it has been difficult for African Americans to win elected judgeships. The appointive process, with recommendations from the area's dominant political party, provides an avenue to fill some of these seats with minorities and female justices. Currently in New York City there are 42 judgeships in "violation of the rights of minority voters living in Bronx, Brooklyn and Manhattan" (Wise, 1994, p. 1). What is so ironic is that the Manhattan borough has an African American Democratic political chairman, who would be in the best position to make recommendations to a Democratic governor. However, with the 1994 elections, the New York State governor is a Republican. Therefore, the appointive process, if eligible to continue, might be handicapped by differences in political ideology.

Since 1852, when Robert Morris became the first African American to hold judicial office, judgeships have not come easily to African American candidates. Whatever process is open to them, be it appointive or elective, these judgeships have to be sought with vigor and determination.

As we have seen, studies have indicated that there exist within the criminal justice system opportunities for those in charge of handing out punishments (for example, police officers) to let racism cloud their judgment. Each day in the United States the courts process an endless parade of African Americans. If African American judges are to make a difference, their numbers must increase. Meanwhile, the New York City court system has, in its appointive process, used this window of opportunity to increase the number of women and minorities in its criminal courts. A concern is that, with so few windows of opportunity afforded to African Americans (both legal and professional), those who are appointed to judgeships must be particularly sensitive to the communities in which they serve.

Chapter 10

International Corrections and Women of Color

As a leader in the international community, the United States is vested with the authority as the defender of democracy and the disciplinary force for those who violate human rights. While America mediates the problems of the world, its prison walls continue to swell with large numbers of incarcerated blacks and Hispanic women. Not only does the United States mediate the problems of Third World countries but it also provides them with resources to help their economies. The Middle Eastern countries get the bulk of the aid: in 1994 Israel received $3.0 billion, Egypt $2.1 billion, Turkey $590 million, and Greece $310 million. (El Salvador was next receiving $140 million.) Foreign aid totalled $13.4 billion; by comparison elementary, secondary and vocational education was allotted $14.7 billion, farm subsidies $14.2 billion, and veterans' benefits and services $36.7 billion in the same year.

As foreign countries look to U.S. leadership in foreign affairs and resources, they also look to the U.S. criminal justice system as a model to be emulated. In this chapter I will investigate the treatment of women of color in Canada, Pakistan, Africa, and England to see if they are treated as harshly as in the United States.

Minorities in Canada: Aboriginal or Native and Black Slaves

As in the United States, individuals who first colonized Canada were recruited from among the less desirables of the country from whence they came (ex-convicts and others who were attempting to escape oppression from the British or French governments). Fairly often crimes were committed by females, and it was not uncommon for women to receive harsh treatment, such as public whipping or hanging. As Canadian society matured, white women were viewed as virtuous, gentle, and nurturers of the family. Behavior outside these norms, and those of the church, yielded serious consequences. Like the early settlers of the U.S. colonies, when the French and English arrived in Canada they found that it was inhabited by native Indians (more commonly referred to as aboriginal or first people).

Canada also imported African slaves, but not on as large a scale as their neighbor to the south. Canada's economic base was very different than that of America; therefore, they relied more on and preferred to use Indian (Panes or Pawnus) slaves rather than African slaves (Winks, 1971, p. 9). As far as records are available, we can estimate that by 1759 there were 3,604 slaves in Canada. The slave-master relationship, although it could be cruel, was different from that of the American slave master. Slaves in Canada were allowed to receive certain religious sacraments of confirmation, were baptized, and in some instances the slave owner would serve as godfather to his slave children. Slaves were also allowed to marry, something unheard of in America, where the prohibition served as a means to prevent any sense of family commitment. At one point in Canadian slave history, African slaves were actually allowed to return to their homeland of Sierre Leone. It was not until America's African slaves started entering Canada that the ugliness of racial prejudice began to emerge, and, in direct correlation, the notion of negro inferiority began to take its insidious place in Canadian society.

Canadian Slaves and Their Treatment

The first slave to be reported as jailed in Canada was in 1851. However, it was in Toronto in 1859 that out of 3,232 prisoners we actually can account for 117 blacks; and of the 1,057 women there were 8 black females (Winks, 1971, p. 249). One of the first reported incidents of cruel treatment of a female slave was in 1734. This female slave, known as Angelique, was accused of setting fire to her mistress's house, a fire that spread to 46 other homes in Montreal. When she was captured, a rope was placed around her neck while she held a two-pound burning torch, standing in front of a church. As she kneeled, handcuffed to a post, she was tortured and then burned alive (Boyer, 1966, p. 127). Although black slave life in Canada was different, cruelty toward them by Canadian whites served as the forerunner for other, more subtle forms of prejudice experienced by Canada's people of color.

Canadian Women Prisoners

In ways similar to the early treatment of jailed American women, the Canadian women prisoners were treated no differently than male prisoners. Women were stripped to the waist and whipped, hanged, or sent to a life of hard prison labor. During the eighteenth and nineteenth centuries, incarceration was the preferred punishment, when compared to public humiliation and whipping. When incarcerated, women and children were sent to crowded small prison cells. Fortunately, Canadian women prisoners were blessed with Elizabeth Fry,* who, like the American women's rights' crusaders, took on the government and criticized it for its treatment of female prisoners. The results of her efforts in 1835 helped to secure separate accommodations at Kingston Prison. Women inmates were few in numbers: in 1838 there were 6; in 1845 there were 14; and in 1847 there were 106. However, they did not escape abuse by prison staff and were flogged when they broke prison rules. The next prison for women—Fullen Street Female Prison—opened in 1874 in Montreal. Like the first American prison for women, Fullen Street Female Prison was not built for the welfare of the prisoner but to ease the overcrowding. Andrew Mercer Reformatory for Women was established in 1880 and located in Toronto, Ontario. In 1934 females were moved into prisons for women, which are now reported to be slated for closing (Correctional Services Canada, April 1990). It was also recommended in this report that five regional prisons be built in their place.

Canada's responsibility for women prisoners is divided among the federal, provisional, and territorial governments. Provisional and territorial governments incarcerate women serving less than two years. As in the United States, many Canadian women prisoners are usually housed in locations miles away from their loved ones, making family visits difficult.

*Special thanks are given to the Elizabeth Fry Society, Ottawa, for providing reference material.

Table 10.1 Imprisonment Rate by Country
Per 100,000 Total Population (Adults and Children)

United States	330.00*
Hungary	146.00***
Canada	129.60**
United Kingdom	92.10***
Spain	91.80***
Austria	87.50***
France	83.90***
Portugal	82.00***
Italy	60.50***

The U.S. Department of Justice, Statistics, December 1992. The imprisonment rate is based on an incarcerated population of 847,271. This figure includes all inmates in federal and state prisons, including juveniles tried in adult courts. This figure, however, does not include persons detained in local jails.

**Adult correctional services in Canada, Canadian Center for Justice Statutes 1992–93 (p. 5).*

***Council of Europe, September 1, 1991.*

Source: *Correction in Canada*, 1993, p. 4.

One of the measurements that could be used to discern whether or not a nation has adequate control of its human resources is the rate at which it incarcerates its citizens. According to the 1993 edition of *Correction in Canada*, it was reported that the United States is the leading nation in the incarceration of its citizens (see Table 10.1).

Canadian women prisoners are distributed by region (Atlantic, Quebec, Ontario, Prairies, and Pacific) in one of the regional prisons. The number of women incarcerated in Canada is small when compared to the United States. However, the overrepresentation of aboriginal women, like African American women, is large in relation to their numbers in the general population (aboriginal, 3 percent; African American, 11 percent). Correctional Services Canada (Federally Sentenced Women Initiative Booklet, undated) notes that "There are approximately 330 women serving federal sentences. Aboriginal women are over-represented in the federal prison system and make up approximately 17 percent of incarcerated women."

This disparity was also reported to be more pronounced by region (see Table 10.2).

Table 10.2 Percentage of Canadian
Unregistered Offenders by Race and Region, 1992-93*

	Atl.	Que.	Ont.	Pra.	Pac.
White	100	90.8	73.7	40.4	63.8
Aboriginal	0	1.5	9.6	55.8	19.1
Black	0	6.2	9.0	0	6.4
Asiatic	0	0	2.6	0	2.1
Other	0	1.5	5.1	3.8	8.5

*Represents 323 females.

Source: *Correction in Canada*, 1993 edition, p. 20.

Another way of looking at the data is to compare the minority population data with the nonminority, white population (see Table 10.3).

As you can see, the Prairie region has the highest rates of incarceration of aboriginal women (unadjusted), despite the fact that they represent only 11 percent of the population in the region (Canadian Association Elizabeth Fry, February 20, 1993). When the minority data are combined, the Prairie region's overrepresentation percentage of minority offenders is still the highest, followed by the Pacific and Ontario regions, respectively.

Canadian women offenders, like U.S. women, tend to fall heavily into crimes that are poverty-driven: namely drugs, prostitution, and robbery (see Table 10.4).

Of these females, 78 percent had no previous federal term of incar-

Table 10.3 Percentage of
Canadian Registered Offenders by Race and Region
1992-93 (Revised Data as reported)

	Atl.	Que.	Ont.	Pra.	Pac.
Nonminority	100	90.8	73.7	40.4	63.8
Minority*	0	9.2	26.3	59.6	36.1

*Includes aboriginal, black, Asiatic, and others.

Source: *Corrections in Canada*, 1993 edition, p. 20.

Table 10.4 Types of Offenses of Canadian Registered Female Federal Offenders, 1992-93

Drugs	21.1
Robbery	17.3
Homicide	18.6
Manslaughter	10.2
Other nonviolent offenses	18.9

Source: Adapted from *Correction in Canada*, 1993 edition, p. 28.

ceration, while 13.3 had at least one previous term of imprisonment. The annual cost to keep an offender in a federal institution in 1992-93 was $47,760 (*Corrections in Canada*, 1993, p. 48).

The aboriginal woman of Canada has suffered the degradation of society similar to that experienced by the African American female slave. Forced to leave her home, she was then relegated to a life on a reserve where her children were ripped from her arms and placed in residential schools where they were made to learn European ideals and values. Here their own cultural values and skills of hunting, fishing, and trapping became less and less a part of each succeeding generation. Upon reaching adulthood, by virtue of the 1985 Indian Act, she was denied the right to live on the reserve if she married a nonnative.

Poorly educated or miseducated, with health problems due to the conditions on the reserve, this female now seeks refuge in urban areas. Once there the reality of urban life, which fails to employ her or her mate, make her easy prey for drugs, alcohol, prostitution, and the violence that leads to incarceration. Prison data confirms that 90 percent of the aboriginal women who are in federal prisons have histories of physical abuse and 61 percent are victims of sexual abuse. Thus, the cycle of abuse, where the abused becomes the abuser, is perpetuated for generations. Unless the cycle is broken, the prison walls will continue to swell with poor aboriginal and other subjugated minority women.

Africa's Treatment of Women

Africa, like many Third World countries, has been keenly involved with severing its ties to European and Asian countries that were

responsible for colonization. Because of this, these people find themselves in a continuous struggle to free themselves, to bring professional
doctors for hospitals, scholars and professors for their university depart-
ments (especially social sciences), and to develop organized systems of
criminal justice. In addition, "African countries lack national statistical data collection systems to provide the base for scientific research
and planning" (Arthur, 1991, p. 499). However, Human Rights and
Amnesty International are two international organizations that serve
as a watchful eye on the treatment of women in Third World countries
and have been used as a major source for the author's needed insight
into the treatment of African, Pakistani, and other Third World
women.

African Women and the Law

Overall, South African prison conditions mirrored the treatment
of African American slaves and the early American prison system,
where prisoners were brutalized, segregated, and sentenced to death
row. Specific laws regarding the segregation of black and white female
prisoners were strictly enforced. In fact, the law read thus: "as far as possible, white and nonwhite prisoners shall be detained in separate parts
thereof and in such manner as to prevent white and nonwhite prisoners from being within view of each other; and wherever practicable,
nonwhite prisoners of different races shall be separated" (Africa Watch,
1994, p. 1). Since the dismantling of apartheid, this has begun to change,
as will be discussed later. This segregated system also spilled over into
every aspect of the prison system. In the personnel area, whites and
blacks were hired as guards; however, white prisoners were guarded by
white prison guards. Africa Watch (1994) reported that since the end
of apartheid and its visit to South Africa "most prisons still had their
traditional racial profiles, with only a small proportion of inmates of
other races" (p. 17). It was further reported that at the women's Kroon-
stead Prison out of 147 prisoners 32 were white, 99 were black, and 16
were colored (mixed race).

Like the United States, white-ruled South Africa experienced an
overwhelming prison population of oppressed blacks. On December 31,
1992, the South African prison population was reported by Africa
Watch, Division of Human Rights Watch, to be as follows: white, 4,258
(of which 191 were women); and nonwhite, 104,440 (of which 3,178

were women). In addition, the nonwhite population was subdivided into Asian (586), Indian ancestry; colored (27,315); mixed race and black (76,448) (p. 17). The sentencing process and the crimes for which these women had been sentenced is difficult to obtain. As previously mentioned, statistical data are not developed and reported as in Western countries. Nevertheless, it has been reported (Adler, 1981; Biles, 1988) that, in some African counties, women's crimes include political offenses, armed robbery, kidnapping children,* shoplifting, other thefts, prostitution, and murder. Once a female is imprisoned she is assigned to one of South Africa's privileged groups of A, B, C, or D.

Where she is assigned within the alphabetical grouping has nothing to do with her crime or the level of danger she presents. Rather she starts at C and works her way up to the A level. This system is extremely harsh and her children can only visit her when she reaches A level. Most of these women never have a chance to visit with their children, due to the slowness of the progression from level C to A, and often the woman's sentence is of such duration that she is discharged before reaching level A. For example, in 1992, of the 241 sentenced prisoners at Pollsmoor, "there were 27 group A inmates; 38 group B; 172 group C, and 4 group D" (Africa Watch, 1994, p. 25). Also, "the prison system in which she must live is segregated and riddled with abuse." The system allows women with children of up to two years of age, and in some case to four years, to keep the children with them in prison. "As of May 1993 there were 189 children under 4 years of age in the prisons" (Africa Watch, 1994, p. 72). Similar to the United States, those women who are lucky enough to receive vocational training are usually steered into typical occupations such as hairdressers. Unfortunately, they are few in number: out of the 2,581 prisoners receiving vocational training in June 1991 only 9 were female (p. 73). Those prisoners who do not have a clean record while in prison often receive reduced meals, isolation, and physical or corporal punishments. Africa Watch did not specifically note the disciplinary actions taken against females; however an abuse system without parameters has no conscience, and so punishments have no gender limitations.

The injustice of South Africa's years of apartheid has permeated every level of its criminal justice system. Therefore, the abuse that female prisoners have endured will continue until the prison system can

---

*In some African cultures childless females are considered inferior; therefore childstealing is a crime that women commit.

be overhauled, which will, more than likely, take years. With the imposition of minimum standards—supported and adopted by the United
Nations with the treatment of prisoners as a guide—the South African
prison system can improve its deplorable treatment of women inmates.

Punishment of Women Prisoners in Pakistan

African American and Pakistani women share similar harsh experiences due to their gender and their position in the social structure of
their country. As such, these Pakistanis are subjected to some of their
government's most discriminatory practices, resulting in their incarceration.

Women who are educated, upper class, and live in urban areas
have a much better life. Like the African American woman slave, "the
average rural woman of Pakistan is born in near slavery, leads a life of
drudgery and dies in oblivion" ("Report of Pakistan Commission on the
Status of Women," 1981, p. 31). The majority (75 percent) of women in
Pakistan live in rural communities, work 16–18 hours per day, and bear
at least eight children. Likewise, as with the African American slaves,
they will have a high maternal mortality rate, be illiterate, and live in
poverty with their children. It is extremely difficult to discuss the
women of Pakistan without mentioning the struggle they have had
with religious ideology and women's rights.

In a country like Pakistan sexism intermingles with religion and
cultural concerns, and these factors have shaped how women are treated
inside and outside the criminal justice system. There are many social
and cultural controls that make women vulnerable and justify their
poor treatment in prison. One method used quite effectively in the
United States and Pakistan to control and justify imprisonment has
been the manipulation of laws to oppress women and keep them in their
social class.

The Hudood Ordinances, an Islamic penal law, criminalizes
(among other things) theft, drunkenness, adultery, deformation, fornication, and rape, and prescribes punishments for these offenses that
include stoning to death, public flogging, and amputation (Asia Watch,
1992, p. 3). Prior to the passage of this law in 1979 there were only 70
Pakistani women incarcerated at the time. Following its passage the
number of imprisoned women jumped to 2,000 by 1991 (p. 3). These
laws, which have their foundation in religious doctrine, have resulted

in imprisoned females being mistreated, and they are now vulnerable to sexual attacks by male guards. These laws, which are clearly gender biased, are discriminatory because they require male corroboration when applied to females. For example, testimony of proof of rape for the maximum punishment of stoning to death or 100 lashes in public (p. 4) must be corroborated by a male, because the testimony of women does not carry any real legal weight. In court she cannot testify against a male who raped her (therefore the perpetrator goes free), and, in some cases, she goes to jail charged with adultery or fornication. To illustrate this injustice, *Asia Watch* and the Women's Rights Project Report (1992) offers the following case: "Eighteen year old Mayluda Mujid was abducted by several men, raped by her abductors over a two-month period, and finally turned over by them to the police. Although she complained that she had been raped, the police charged her with illicit sex, imprisoned her pending trial and let the men go free" (*Asia Watch*, 1992, p. 4).

In addition, in 1989 two nurses were raped at gunpoint by three interns in a Karachi hospital. One of the victims tried to file a complaint and was, herself, charged with admitting to sexual intercourse. As a result of the charges she lost her job and her marital engagement was broken off (Amnesty International, 1992, p. 6).

Women in Pakistan are also incarcerated for crimes other than the Hudood Ordinances. Like poor African American women, Pakistani women are incarcerated for the murder of their husbands. Murder is one of the two major offenses for which these women are sent to prison.

The social control of women through the use of Islamic laws has been used more stringently against poorer women who have gained the least from the efforts of some women's rights' groups to improve their circumstances. Unfortunately, as we have seen with African American women, "the number of women in prison at any given moment—the vast majority of whom are illiterate and impoverished and, therefore, in no position to press for their rights—soared from as few as 70 in 1980 to as many as 4,500 in 1990" (*Asia Watch*, 1992, p. 37). In addition, "Women in Pakistan were treated as possessions rather than self-reliant, self-regulating humans. They are bought, sold, beaten, mutilated and even killed with impunity and social approval. [And] the vast majority are made to work as many as 16 to 18 hours a day without payment" (p. 37).

To reiterate, poor Pakistani women, as is the case of poor women in the United States, constitute the largest number of those incarcerated. However, with the election in 1988 of Benazir Bhutto (the first female prime minister of a Muslin country) some women who were sentenced under the Hudood received amnesty, but those who had not been sentenced (pending sentencing) were not affected (*Asia Watch*, 1992, p. 40).

The number of women has consistently grown under the Hudood alone: in 1983 there were 1,682 women facing trial. These poor women were then subjected to (reported) mistreatment. In a "1988 survey of female prisoners ... 78 percent alleged mistreatment while in police custody and 72 percent claimed they had been sexually abused by police. Sexual abuse ranged from rape, including the insertion of foreign objects into the vagina and rectum, to beating and manipulation of exposed genital area, to stripping and public exposure" (*Asia Watch*, 1992, p. 42).

Pakistani women will continue to be detained and eventually placed in prison by laws that are gender biased and discriminate against them when applied by the Pakistani government, as long as the justice system in that country legalizes its application. The discrimination in Pakistan is not along color lines, as in the United States—white versus black—when laws are applied, but rather in Pakistan it is male versus female. No matter what the basis of discrimination is, someone suffers, and it is usually the one with the least power: blacks or other minorities in the United States and women in Pakistan. When the Pakistani courts reverse a female's charge of rape to a charge against that woman of fornication (which carries a lengthy sentence), this certainly becomes a deterrent for women to accuse the male perpetrator. Discriminatory practices by judges and magistrates are also common (*Asia Watch*, 1992, p. 114) when women are clearly the victims. As reported by a female judge, "women who do not have counsel will rot" (p. 44).

Due to the reported number of Bangladeshi females brought into Pakistan each year who are sold into a life of servitude or prostitution, the rights of many females are violated prior to and during their confinement (Amnesty International, 1992). This form of slavery—where as many as 100 girls as young as 15 years of age are sold to the highest bidder each month—has set the stage for another tragic episode in the history of slavery. The U.S. lesson should serve as a reminder that slavery cannot solve the problems of a weak and frail government.

Female Prisoners of Color in England and Wales

England's participation in the African slave trade is well documented in the literature. England, which is now home for many descendants of

African (Afro-Caribbean) women who migrated there in large numbers following World War II, is one of England's largest ethnic groups.
As more women of color found their way to Great Britain and began
to work, white, Anglo-Saxon citizens began to believe that these
African descendants were stealing their jobs. Thus we begin to see
experiences similar to those in the United States: women who are forced
to seek other means (theft, drug trafficking) to support themselves and
their families. When the economic constraints of a country become
problematic those citizens who are the least prepared educationally or
vocationally fall prey to those willing to take advantage of them.

England's ethnic and racial minorities include West Indian,
Guyanese, African (which will hereafter be referred to as black), Indian,
Pakistani, Bangladeshi; and Chinese, Arak, and those of mixed origin.
Are these groups exploited and therefore a large segment of the British
prison population? Beverly Bryan, Stella Dodzie, and Susanne Scafe
reported in 1985 that "In some prisons, where up to 40 percent of the
women inmates can be black, ... (and like other poor women of color)
most black women are there for 'economic' crimes such as shoplifting,
prostitution, selling ganja or passing stolen cheques" (p. 120). Prison
statistics from the British Home Office began to be published in 1986
regarding race and ethnic makeup of its female prison population. In
the following year the Women's Prison Resource Center (WPRC) also
noticed that in 1987, 34 percent of their referrals from prison were for
black inmates. WPRC began to provide referrals or links for inmates
seeking housing, education, employment, welfare, and drug programs
outside the prison. The Black Female Prisoner's Scheme also provided
referral services (for example, education, housing, welfare, and social
activities for ex-offenders) (Thomas-Crando, 1988).

With these organizations and others that recognized the large
numbers of black female prisoners in Great Britain, a review of prison
data helped to validate and verify this suspicion. A review of the Home
Office Statistical Report found that the majority of the women were
being sentenced to prison terms for crimes related to economics. In 1988
the Home Office reported that crimes committed overall by females
involved drugs, theft, and violence against a person (Home Office
Report, 1988, Table 5.3, p. 101). A closer look at crimes for 199 women
by ethnic origin revealed that drug, theft, and other offenses were committed by black females. Most noticeable and troubling is the upward
progression of the sentencing length for black women to white women,
(see Table 10.5).

Table 10.5 All Sentenced Females by
Ethnicity in England and Wales, 1985–91
(Sentences over 18 Months, Including Life)

Year	Total Whites Sentenced	3 Years to Life Terms	Total Blacks Sentenced	3 Years to Life Terms
1985	934	242	133	52
1986	975	337	141	45
1987*	1,036	393	239	153
1988*	902	420	249	178
1989*	890	438	276	210
1990*	824	399	305	239
1991*	767	385	278	214

*Home Office Report, Prison Statistics: England and Wales, 1991, Table 1.13, p. 36.

Source: Home Office Report, Prison Statistics: England and Wales, 1989, Table 1.13, p. 35.

Is there a disparity in the sentencing of black women? In 1991, according to the Home Office Report, of the 674 sentenced adult white women 142 had committed violence against a person, 128 theft, 102 drug offenses, 74 other; yet 385 received sentences of over 18 months. Of the 261 adult black women who were sentenced 11 committed violence against a person, 31 theft, 125 drug offenses, and 66 other offenses. Of that number 214 received sentences of over 18 months (see tables 1.12 and 1.13). Based upon this data, it appears that black women committed less violent crimes than white women, but more drug-related offenses, for which they were apparently given stiffer sentences. While the analysis of the data is limited, and there was only a mere sampling of black women, the status of women of color in the British criminal justice system does raise concerns of equity.

In conclusion, our neighbor to the north, Canada, can also be credited with the unfair treatment of aboriginal and native women. These Indian women, who as children were uprooted from their homeland, were pushed into residential schools, where their culture and ethnicity were not among the lessons they learned. Forced off the reservations if they married a non–Indian or tried to find employment, they found a foreign, urban community that exploited their naivete and their sexuality. This resulted in these women eventually breaking the law and being confined to a prison far away from their homes. While imprisoned, the criminal justice system further sapped their energy without replacing it with usable or marketable skills upon release. As Canada takes its third position below the United States in rates of incarceration, it plans to close prisons for women and open five new provisional prisons and a Healing Lodge for its large population of incarcerated aboriginal females. Alternatives to incarceration should also assume some of the Canadian government's attention.

Third World countries like South Africa, which has been embroiled in civil war and apartheid, will need years to build a criminal justice system that treats fairly its African and minority female prisoners. Other countries, like Pakistan, exploit their female prisoners under the guise of religion and the female's position in that culture. Their exploitation and treatment by male guards and wardens has been documented by Amnesty International and Africa and Pakistan Watch. A watchful eye by international groups on the treatment of women prisoners who call for stricter compliance with international standards is the Third World female's only salvation. And finally, British statistics point to the overrepresentation of blacks and other ethnic groups in British prisons. Although black women appear to commit fewer violent crimes, it appears that they are given longer sentences than their white counterparts who commit larger numbers of violent crimes. Black women and other ethnic group members are, as reported in 1991, more involved in drug trafficking.

While data (statistics) from Third World countries are sketchy or nonexistent, what we know is that equity in sentencing and treatment issues need to be seriously addressed.

Chapter 11

Conclusions and
Recommendations

When I began my research for this book some four years ago, I had no idea about the magnitude of the inequitable treatment of African American female prisoners in a country that is founded on democracy, equality, and justice for all. This country treats its women prisoners, whose ancestors suffered 400 years of horrifying experiences, as if they were space aliens. But these people continue to love this nation, even though each day in U.S. courts blacks are herded into the modern type of plantation—prisons—where they are subjected to unthinkable experiences. Our U.S. criminal justice system is an outgrowth of the social thinking and structure of this nation and can only be changed if the social structure that supports this thinking is altered.

My exposure to the U.S. criminal justice system has resulted in the following recommendations, which I believe could begin to help create an environment that this nation could consider to heal a dying system. These recommendations are by no means all-inclusive, and they only serve as a beginning for discussion and consideration by correction and governmental officials.

1. Recommendation:

Meaningful and transferable skills and training for prisoners.

Rationale:

To control recidivism among state African American female prisoners they must receive meaningful education, coupled with skill training while incarcerated. With the increasing number of women

Table 11.1 Age and Education
of State Female Prisoners, 1991, in Percentages

Age	*Percent*	*Education*	*Percent*
18–24	16.3	8th grade	16.0
25–34	50.4	Some high school	45.8
35–44	25.5	High school	22.7

Source: Adapted from Table I, p. 2, U.S. Department of Justice, Bureau of Justice Statistics Special Report, Survey of State Prison Inmates, 1991.

entering prisons (see Table 11.1) who are young and lack a high school diploma, prison education must seize the opportunity to eliminate illiteracy.

According to a number of published accounts (Simon and Landes, 1991; Ryan, 1984) vocational programs were typically gender-specific (for example, laundry, data entry, typing) training. Therefore, training programs should be developed that provide meaningful employment opportunities. Programs for African American female inmates should first be Afro-centric with a foundation in teaching pride in cultural heritage. These programs could be developed to teach or enhance reading skills, and build pride and self-esteem. The vocational skill component should provide training that prepares prisoners to compete for jobs in a global economy (for example, on the information superhighways), training that will be more technical and challenging that provides for employment opportunities and job stability. Health careers should also be considered for those inmates who are eligible to participate in certain training, leading to certification and licensure (for example, nursing, medical technology, radiology technology). Since the healthcare industry will continue to grow and require skilled personnel, prison education officials should consider exploring these career options (also see AIDS recommendations).

2. Recommendation:
House arrest for women prisoners infected with the AIDS virus.

Rationale:
According to the U.S. Department of Justice Special Report of State Prison Inmates, 54 percent of these new prisoners had used drugs the month before their arrest. This exposure to drugs places these

women at risk of having contacted the AIDS virus either through shared infected needles or prostitute behavior to pay for their habit. Further, this study revealed that 42 percent of white women, 46 percent of Hispanic women, and 24 percent of black women used injectable drugs. Of those women tested for the AIDS virus in state prisons, as reported by this 1991 survey, 1.9 percent of whites tested positive, 6.8 percent of Hispanics, and 3.5 percent of black women (p. 9). These prisoners, who will eventually become ill, should be, if the offense allows, considered for house arrest. The inmate who is ill could then receive services by Hospice agencies and supervision in the community. This would free prison space and resources, and keep inmates in their community where their family could care for them in their final days. A Hospice program that serves inmates with AIDS on house arrest could also serve as a potential training site and employer of inmates who are receiving skill training before being released to their communities. This last aspect of the recommendation would need further study to assure that all state and department of corrections and parole laws are not violated.

3. Recommendation:
Expand child visitation with the incarcerated mother.

Rationale:
In the 1991 U.S. Department of Justice survey of inmates it was stated that two-thirds of the women had at least one child younger than 18 years of age. This translates into 56,000 minor children. Of these 56,000 children, 69 percent of the black and 72 percent of the Hispanic children had lived with their mother prior to her arrest. Further, it was stated that 46 percent of the mothers had talked to the child by telephone; 45 percent had weekly mail contact; and a meager 9 percent had actually been visited by their children. These visits were unlikely to help to provide the nurturing that young children need.

Therefore, prison officials should devise scheduling procedures that would increase visitation and congregate visitation that would help to foster lasting bonds between mother and child.

4. Recommendation:
Provide a defendant advocate (court advocate) for each case.

Rationale:
Some judicial systems have explored the use of a courtroom advocate that would serve as a liaison between the female offender and the

judge. The impartial liaison would gather valuable information for consideration by the judge.

The offender advocate would agree to help supervise the offender, who may be released to an advocate program like WHRD (discussed in Chapter 8) or on limited house arrest.

5. Recommendation:

Expand the use of technology to permit house arrest for women offenders who have small children.

Rationale:

Where possible, the use of electronic technology should be used as an alternative to imprisonment. This option could be most useful for women offenders who have small children. (As reported in 1991, there were 56,000 children under 18 years whose mothers were incarcerated.) Eligible prisoners could be monitored by leg devices. This would allow the women to see their children off to school and prepare for their return.

This also provides the opportunity for the inmate-mother to utilize the television Network Distance Learning option to complete her GED or take college courses. The children of the house-arrest female inmates could see their mothers in a more positive environment and foster a closer nurturing relationship.

At a time when corrections should be addressing recidivism rates, they are faced with conservative lawmakers who are proposing, over a four-year period, cuts of $57 million for food stamps, housing programs, and similar programs that serve poor women and children. These cuts could force more women onto the streets and into a life of crime as a means of supporting themselves and their children.

6. Recommendation:

Parenting classes for inmates.

Rationale:

According to the Department of Justice 1991 study, Table 17, 6.7 percent of blacks, 5.2 percent of whites, and 5.9 percent of Hispanics are pregnant at the time of their incarceration. With so many inmates who have children under 18 years of age, coupled with those who will deliver while incarcerated, it would be the natural place to begin to teach parenting skills. Parenting classes should focus on child-care skills and foster nurturing abilities.

7. Recommendation:

Increase in African American female and other ethnic correctional officers.

Rationale:

The modern correctional officer should be prepared to deal with a new inmate who, in most cases, does *not* look like his sister or wife. For she is a minority, young, uneducated, sick, and tired of being abused on the streets, according to the Department of Justice June 1993 yearbook. White males (115,443) are the major holders of correctional officers' positions. They also make up the majority of corrections personnel (76,788) in adult and juvenile systems. Affirmative action programs need strengthening to assure that not only blacks are given the opportunities to hold these positions, but also women, who make up a meager 31,556 positions (17,527 white; 12,431 black; 1,598 Hispanic). Also, there should be an increase in the number of African Americans who are in high-level warden and superintendent positions. There are 950 white, 150 black, and 43 Hispanic male wardens and superintendents (U.S. Department of Justice, Sourcebook, 1993).

An increase in minority officers should bring with it the sensitivities of their culture. Other nonminority correctional staff must have specific cultural diversity training. There should be state incentives offered to those correctional officers who participate in cultural sensitivity workshop training sessions and practice what is taught. Prison rehabilitation programs that work will reduce recidivism and enhance correctional officer and inmate relations, thus reducing safety risks. Because there is hope and hope will impact, positively, on female inmate institutional behavior, common sense tells us that this would work in favor of those who want and need it.

8. Recommendation:

Expansion of health service programs for sick inmates.

Rationale:

Female inmates are some of this nation's most sickly citizens (see Chapter 7, and Department of Justice 1991 study). Large numbers of inmates received medication from psychiatrists and other doctors for emotional problems (17.8 percent white; 14.2 percent black; and 12.1 percent Hispanic). Of these women, 17.5 percent of the white women were admitted for treatment, while 7.7 percent of the black and 6.5 percent of the Hispanic were admitted. Prison health resources must be made available to repair the damage that has resulted from years without physicals, PAP smears, or mammograms, and years of prostitution and battering from pimps and drug pushers.

As we have noted in a number of the chapters in this book, prison health personnel must be trained and available to screen and treat inmates.

Bibliography

Adams, Stewart. "The Black-Shift Phenomenon in Criminal Justice." *Justice System Journal* (Winter 1976, Vol. 2), 185–194.

Adamson, C. "Punishment after Slavery: Southern State Penal System 1859–1895." *Social Problems* (June 1983).

Adler, Freda. *Sisters in Crime: The Rise of the New Female Criminal.* New York: McGraw-Hill, 1975.

The Incidence of Female Criminality in the Contemporary World. New York: New York University Press, 1981.

Adler, Freda and Rita Simon, eds. *The Criminology of Deviant Women.* Boston: Houghton Mifflin, 1979.

Africa Watch. *Prison Conditions in South Africa.* New York: Division of Human Rights Watch, 1994.

American Civil Liberties Union. Memorandum (July 1994), Laura Murphy Lee, Washington, D.C.

American Correctional Association (ACA). *The Female Offender: What Does the Future Hold?* Washington, D.C.: St. Mary's, 1990.

Amnesty International. "Rape and Sexual Abuse: Torture and Ill-Treatment of Women in Detention." (1992). New York.

Arnold, Regina. "Process of Victimization and Criminalization of Black Women." In Barbara Price and Natalie J. Sokoloff, *The Criminal Justice System and Women Offenders, Victims, and Workers.* New York: McGraw-Hill, 1995.

Arthur, John. "Development and Crime in Africa: A Test of Modernization Theory." *Journal of Criminal Justice* 19 (1991): 499–513.

Asia Watch Committee (U.S.) Women Rights Project, Human Rights Watch. "Double Jeopardy—Police Abuse of Women in Pakistan." (1992). New York.

Avery, Byllye. "The Health Status of Black Women." In R. Braithwaite and S.E. Taylor, eds., *Health Issues in the Black Community.* San Francisco: Jossey-Bass, 1992.

Barkan, Steven, and Steven Cohn. "Racial Prejudice and Support for the Death Penalty by Whites." *Journal of Research in Crime and Delinquency* 31, no. 2 (May 1994): 202–9.

Baunach, P. J. "You Can't Be a Mother and Be in Prison ... Can You? Impacts of the Mother-Child Separation" In Barbara R. Price and Natalie Sokoloff, *Criminal Justice System and Women*. New York: Clark Boardman (1982), 155–169.

Beardsley, Edward. "Race as a Factor in Health." In Rima Apple, ed., *Women, Health and Medicine in America: A Historical Handbook*. New York: Garland, 1990.

Becnel, B. "The Crime-Unemployment Cycle." *AFL-CIO Report* (November 1978).

Bell, D. A. "Racism in American Court: Cause for Black Disproportion or Despair?" *California Law Review* (January 1973): 165–203.

Biles, David, ed. *Current International Trends in Corrections*. Washington, D.C.: Federal Press, 1988.

Black Issues in Higher Education. Book review of *Robes On, Gloves Off* by Raymond Brown, June 29, 1995: 32.

Blumberg, M. "Transmission of the AIDS Virus." *Commercial Law Bulletin* 25, no. 5 (September-October 1989): 454–65.

Boudouris, J. "Prison and Kids, Program for Inmate Parents." *American Correctional Association*. College Park, Md., 1985.

Braithwaite, John. "The Future of Prisons—A Canadian View." In David Biles, ed. *Current International Trends in Corrections*. Washington, D.C.: Federation Press, 1988.

Bresler, Lewis, and Diane Lewis. "Black and White Women Prisoners' Differences in Family Ties and Their Programmatic Implications." *Prison Journal* 63, no. 2 (1983): 116–123.

Bryan, Beverly, Stella Dodzie, and Susanne Scafe. *Heart of the Race: Black Women's Lives in Britain*. London: Verago, 1985.

Browker, L. H. *Women, Crime and the Criminal Justice System*. Lexington, Mass.: Lexington Books, 1978.

Buffalo News, October 5, 1994; November 13, 1994; January 19, 1995; September 11, 1995; September 25, 1996.

Canadian Association Elizabeth Fry (CAEF). February 20, 1993.

Carlen, Pat. *Alternatives to Women's Imprisonment*. Philadelphia: Open University Press, 1990.

Centers for Disease Control. *HIV/AIDS Surveillance Report* Atlanta: CDC, Vol. 8, no. 1 (June 1996).

Center for the Study of Criminology and Law. University of Florida.

The (Buffalo, N.Y.) *Challenger*. "Death of Ben Vereen's Sister Probed," March 27, 1996: 4.

Congressional Digest (June-July 1994).

Corrections in Canada. *Basic Facts About Corrections in Canada*. (1993A).

_____. *Creating Choices: The Report on the Task Force on Federally Sentenced Women*. (April 1990).

_____. *Federally Sentenced Women Initiative Brochure*. (1993B).

Cowie, J., V. Cowie, and C. Slater. *Delinquency in Girls*. Cambridge, Mass.: Humanities Press, 1968.

Crites, Laura. *The Female Offender*. Lexington, Mass.: Lexington Books, 1976.

_____. *Women Offenders: Myths vs. Reality.* Lexington, Mass.: Lexington Books, 1978.

Crockett, George W. "The Role of the Black Judge." *The Criminal Justice System and Blacks.* New York: Clark Boardman, 1984.

Crown, Herman L. "A Political History of the Texas Penal System 1829–1951." Dissertation, University of Texas, 1964.

C-SPAN. House Judiciary Subcommittee Hearing. January 19, 1995(A).

C-SPAN. State of California. Attorney General, Daniel Lungren. January 19, 1995(B).

Datesman, Susan, and Gloria Cales. "I'm Still the Same Mommy: Maintaining the Mother/Child Relationship in Prison." *The Prison Journal* 63(2) (1983): 142–154.

Davis, Abraham. *Blacks in the Federal Judiciary.* Bristol, Ind.: Wyndham Hall, 1989.

Day, Phyllis. *A New History of Social Welfare.* Englewood Cliffs, N.J.: Prentice-Hall, 1989.

"Death Penalty Sentencing: Research Indicates Patterns of Racial Disparities." U.S. General Accounting Office. GAO/GGD-90-57. (February 1990).

Decker, John F. "Prostitution as a Public Health Issue." In *AIDS and the Law*, editors, Scott Burris and Harlon L. Dalton. New Haven, Conn.: Yale University Press, 1987.

De Zalduondo, Barbara. "Prostitution Views Cross Culturally Towards Recontextualizing Sex Work in AIDS Intervention Research." *Journal of Sex Research* 28, no. 2 (May 1991): 223–48.

Di Nitto, Dione, and Thomas Dye. *Social Welfare Politics and Public Policy.* Englewood Cliff, N.J.: Prentice-Hall, 1987.

Dunsten, Alfred Bishop. *The Black Man in the Old Testament and Its World.* Philadelphia: Dorrance, 1974.

Ebony. "Crisis in the Black Family," May 1986.

Ethridge, Philip, and James Marquart. "Private Prisons in Texas: The New Penology for Profit." *Justice Quarterly* 10, no. 1 (March 1993): 29–47.

Feinman, Clarice. "An Historical Overview of the Treatment of Incarcerated Women: Myths and Realities of Rehabilitation." *Prison Journal* 63, no. 2 (1984): 12–26.

_____. *Women in the Criminal Justice System.* 2d ed. New York: Praeger, 1986.

Flowers, B. Ronald. *Women and Criminality: The Woman as Victim, Offender and Practitioner.* Westport, Conn.: Greenwood, 1987.

_____. *Demographics: The Characteristics of Crime in America.* Westport, Conn.: Greenwood, 1989.

_____. *Minorities and Criminality.* Westport, Conn.: Greenwood, 1990.

Foley, L. A., and C. E. Rasche. "Effect of Race on Sentence, Actual Time Served and Final Disposition of Female Offender." In *Theory Research in Criminal Justice: Current Perspectives.* Cincinnati: Anderson, 1979.

Freedman, Estelle. *Their Sister's Keepers: A Historical Perspective of Female Correctional Institutes in the U.S. 1870–1900.* Feminist Studies 2(1) (1974): 77–95.

_____. *Their Sister's Keepers: Women's Prison Reforms in America, 1830–1930*. Ann Arbor: University of Michigan Press, 1981.

French, L. "An Assessment of the Black Female Prisoner in the South." *Signs: Journal of Women in Culture and Society* 3, no. 2, (Winter 1978): 483–88.

_____. "Incarcerated Black Female—The Case of Social Double Jeopardy." *Journal of Black Studies* 8: 321–35 (March 1978).

_____. "A Profile of the Incarcerated Black Female Offender." *Prison Journal* 3, no. 2 (1983): 80–87.

"Geraldo." January 24, 1995.

Glamour magazine. Editorial, March 1994: 80.

Glick, Ruth, and Virginia Neto. *National Study of Women's Correctional Programs*. Washington, D.C.: National Institute of Law Enforcement and Criminal Justice, Law Enforcement Assistance Administration, U.S. Department of Justice, June 1977.

Glueck, Sheldon, and Eleanore Glueck. *Five Hundred Delinquent Women*. New York: Alfred A. Knopf, 1934.

Godman, Nancy, and Jean Price. *Studies of Female Offenders*. London: Home Office, 1967.

Goldsmith, Barbara. "Women on the Edge." *The New Yorker*, April 26, 1993, 64–81.

Goldstein, Matthew. "Justice Department Challenges 42 Judgeships." *New York Law Journal* (December 1994), p. 1, col 3.

Good Housekeeping. "Grandmothers in Place of Mothers." (July 1994): 181.

Gurnett, Kate. "Use of House Arrest Gaining Popularity." *The* (Albany, N.Y.) *Sunday Gazette*, February 17, 1991: B9.

Hacker, Andrew. *Two Nations: Black and White, Separate, Hostile, Unequal*. New York: Ballantine, 1992.

Henriques, Zelma. "Imprisoned Mothers and Their Children: Separation-Reunion Syndrome Dual Impact." *Women and Criminal Justice*, vol. 8 (1) 1996:77–95.

Hepburn, John. "Race and the Decision to Arrest: An Analysis of Warrants Issued." *Journal of Research in Crime and Delinquency* 15, no. 1 (1978): 54–73.

Hill, Gary, and Elizabeth Crawford. "Women, Race and Crime." *Criminology* 28, no. 4 (1990).

Home Office Report. Prison Statistics: England and Wales. HM Stationery Office (1986, 1988, 1989, 1991).

Huie, Virginia. "Moms in Prison: Where Are the Kids?" *The Progress*. (April 1992), 22–23.

Inglehart, A. "Characteristics of Female Offenders." In J. Fegueria, *Female Prisons in Michigan 1968–1978*. Ann Arbor: University of Michigan Press, 1981.

James, Jennifer. "Prostitution and Prostitutes." In Edward Sagarin and Fred Montanino, eds. *Deviant: Voluntary Actors in a Hostile World*. Morrison, N.J.: General Learning Press, 1977.

Johnson, Byron R., and Paul P. Ross. "The Privatization of Correctional Management: A Review." *Journal of Criminal Justice* 18 (1990): 351–58.

Johnson, Tim. "Diversity and Race Reality and Response." *American Jail.* March-April 1996:9–15.

Klein, D. "The Etiology of Female Crime: A Review of the Literature." *Issues in Criminology* 8, no. 2 (Fall 1973): 3–29.

Kruttschnitt, Candice Marie. "Social Control of Women Offenders—A Study of Sentencing in a Criminal Court." Dissertation, 1979. Yale University.

LEAA (Law Enforcement Assistant Administration). Washington, D.C.: U.S. Department. of Justice, 1976.

Lekkerkerker, Eugenia. *Reformatories for Women in the United States.* Groningen, Netherlands: J. B. Wolters, 1931.

Lewis, Diane. "Black Women Offenders and Criminal Justice—Some Theoretical Considerations." In Marguerite Q. Warren, *Comparing Female and Male Offenders.* Beverly Hills, Calif.: Sage, 1981.

Lewis, Diane and L. Bresler. *Is There a Way Out? A Community Study of Women in the San Francisco Jail.* Washington, D.C.: United States Department of Health Education, and Welfare, 1981.

Lisner, Patricia A. *Pediatric Nursing.* Albany, N.Y.: Delmar, 1983.

Little, Joanne. "The People Set Me Free." *Poverty Law Report* 3 (1975): 1–3.

Lombroso Cesare, and William Ferrero. *The Female Offender* (1895). Reprints, New York: D. Appleton, 1915, 1920.

McCormick, Peter. "Do Women Judges Make a Difference: An Analysis by Court Data." *Canadian Journal of Law and Society.* 8, no. 1 (September 1993): 135–48.

McKelvey, Blake. "American Prisons: A Study in American Social History Prior to 1915." Chicago: University of Chicago Press, 1972.

Mandle, Joan D. "Women, Crime and Social Change." In S. Logary, *New Perspectives on Urban Crime.* Jonesboro, Tenn.: Pilgrimage, 1981.

Mann, Caramel. "Women of Color and the Justice System." In Barbara Price and Natalie Sokolaff's *The Criminal Justice System and Women Offenders, Victims and Workers.* New York: McGraw-Hill, 1995.

Mann, R. "Minority and Female: A Criminal Justice Double Bind." *Social Justice* 16, no. 4 (1988).

Meyers, Marshall. "Police Shooting at Minorities: The Case of Los Angeles." *Annals of the American Academy of Political and Social Sciences* (November 1980): 98–110.

Meyers, Martha. "Social Background and the Sentencing Behavior of Judges." *Criminology* (1988) 26.

Moynahan, J. M. and E. K. Stuart. "The Origin of the American Jail." *Social Issues Resource Series* 2 (1978).

National Association for the Advancement of Colored People (NAACP). In letter dated August 2, 1994. Washington, D.C.: House of Representatives.

National Institute on Drug Abuse (NIDA). (February 1990): (CAP34).

NBC Nightly News. "Report on Death Row Inmates." June 5, 1996.

New York State Department of Health. "HIV/AIDS Epidemiology." April 30, 1995:13.

New York Times. July 9, 1994; December 30, 1994.

"OCA Predicts System Will Manage with Fewer Judges." *New York Law Journal* 1 (December 7, 1994): 3.

Owens, C. E. *Mental Health and Black Offenders.* Lexington, Mass.: D.C. Heath, 1980.

Owens, Charles E., and Jimmy Bell, editors. *Blacks and Criminal Justice.* Lexington, Mass.: D.C. Heath, 1977.

Owens-Cameron, Mary. *The Booster and Snitch: Department Store Shoplifting.* New York: Free Press, 1964.

Pollak, Otto. *The Criminality of Women.* Philadelphia: University of Pennsylvania Press, 1950.

Pollock, Joy. "Early Theories of Female Criminality." In Lee H. Browker, *Women, Crime and the Criminal Justice System.* Lexington, Mass.: Lexington Books, 1978.

Pollock-Byrne, Joycelyn. *Women, Prison and Crime.* Pacific Grove, Calif.: Brooks and Cole, 1990.

Prestin, Terry. "New York Bar Avoids Death Penalty Cases." *New York Lives* (December 30, 1994): 6B.

Price, Barbara Raffel and Natalie J. Sokoloff. *The Criminal Justice System and Women: Offenders, Victims and Workers.* McGraw-Hill, 1995, p. 6.

"Private Prisons in Texas: The New Penology for Profit." *Justice Quarterly* 10, no. 1 (March 1993): 29–45.

Rafter, Nicole. *Partial Justice: State Prisons and Their Inmates 1800–1935.* Boston: Northeastern University, 1985.

Reiman, Jeffery H. *The Rich Get Richer and the Poor Get Prison.* New York: John Wiley and Sons, 1979.

"Report of Pakistan Commission on the Status of Women." Pakistan (1981).

"Report of Pakistan Commission on the Status of Women." Pakistan (1986), 31.

Robinson, L. *Penology in the United States.* Philadelphia: John C. Winston, 1922.

Rogers, Helen Worthington. "A Digest of Laws Establishing Reformatories for Women." In *Journal of Criminal Law, Criminology and Police Science* 13, no. 3 (November 1922): 382–437.

Russell, Deana, and N. Van de Ven. "Crimes Against Women: Proceedings of the International Tribunal." *Les Femmes* (1976).

Russell, Katheryn. "Development of a Black Criminology and the Role of the Black Criminologist." *Justice Quarterly* 9, no. 4 (December 1992).

Ryan, T. A. *Adult Female Offenders and Institutional Programs: State of the Art Analyses.* Washington, D.C.: National Institute of Corrections, 1984.

Schmolling, B. *Human Services in Contemporary America.* Florence, Ky.: Wadsworth, 1992.

Schumen, Congressman Charles. Presentation of "Guide for Community Groups: How to Access the Crime Bill-Prevention Programs." Buffalo, N.Y.: 1995.

Schweber, C. "Beauty Marks and Blemishes: The Cold Prison as a Microcosm of Integrated Society." *Prison Journal* 64, no. 1 (1984): 3–15.

Scutt, Jocelynne A. "Crimes and Equality of the Sexes." *Crime, Punishment and Corrections* 5, no. 1 (1975): 57–69.

Sellin, J. T. *Slavery in the Penal System 1896–1930.* New York: Elsevier, 1976.

Simon, R. J. *Women and Crime.* Lexington, Mass.: D. C. Heath, 1975.

Simon, Rita, and Jean Landes. *The Crimes Women Commit, the Punishments They Receive.* Lexington, Mass.: Lexington Books, 1991.

Smith, David. *Role vs. Robe: The Dilemma of Black Judges.* New York: National University Publication, 1983.

Smith, P., et al. "HIV Infection among Women Entering the New York State Correctional System." *American Journal of Public Health* 81 (1991): 35–39.

Southerland, Edwin H., and Donald R. Cressey. *Criminology,* 9th edition. Philadelphia: Lippincott, 1974.

Spencer, C., and J.C. Berocochea. "Recidivism Among Women Parolees: A Long-Term Survey." In Freda Adler and Rita Simon, *The Criminology of Deviant Women.* Boston: Houghton-Mifflin, 1979.

Spohn, Cassia. "The Sentencing Decisions of Black and White Judges: Expected and Unexpected." *Law and Society Review* 24 (1990): 1216–1997.

Staples, Robert. *The Black Family Essays and Studies.* Belmont, Calif.: Wadsworth, 1994.

Strickland, K. *Correctional Institutions for Women in the United States.* Lexington, Mass.: Lexington Books, 1976.

Swan, L. Alex. *Families of Black Prisoners: Survival and Prayers.* Boston: G.K. Hall, 1981.

Thomas, Jim. *Prisoner Litigation: The Paradox of the Jailhouse Lawyer.* Totowa, N.J.: Rowman and Allanheld, 1988.

Thomas-Crando, J. "Black Female Prisoner's Scheme." *Criminal Justice* 6, no. 3 (1988). London, Howard League.

Thomas, William Isaac. *Sex and Society.* Boston: Little, Brown, 1907.

_____. *The Unadjusted Girl.* Boston: Little, Brown, 1923.

U.S. Census Population. Subject Report: Inmates of Institutions, Females. PC (2-8A, 21; 1960).

U.S. Department of Commerce. Catalog of U.S. Census Population, 1790–1972. June 1974:20.

U.S. Department of Health and Human Services. Third quarter edition. HIV/AIDS (October 1992).

U.S. Department of Health and Human Services, National Institute of Health. "Substance Abuse Among Blacks in the U.S." February 1990:34.

U.S. Department of Justice, Bureau of Justice Statistics, 1986. Historical Corrections Statistics in the United States 1850–1984 by Margret Werner Cahalan. Rockville, MD. NCJ-102529, December 1986, tables 4–5.

U.S. Department of Justice, Bureau of Justice Statistics Special Report. Survey of State Prison Inmates 1991. "Women in Prison," by Tracy Snell.

U.S. Department of Justice. Crime Clock Release, December 4, 1994.

U.S. Department of Justice, Federal Bureau of Prisons. "Race of Females in Federal Prison Facilities as of January 1, 1996." Correspondence with Denise Golvbaski.

U.S. Department of Justice, Federal Bureau of Prisons Office of Research and Evaluation (October 1991, November 1992). Prepared by Sue Kline.

U.S. Department of Justice, Office of Justice Programs, Bureau of Justice Statistics. Sourcebook of Criminal Justice Statistics 1990, 1991, 1993.

U.S. Federal Bureau of Prisons. Research and Evaluation (1991, 1992). Sue Kline correspondence.

U.S. Federal Bureau of Prisons. Research Report. "Black Females in Bureau of Prison Facilities." (October 13, 1991). Prepared by Sue Kline and Patty Garretti.

U.S. General Accounting Office. Washington, D.C. (1979), 8.

U.S. General Accounting Office. "Death Penalty Sentencing: Research Indicates Patterns of Racial Disparities." Washington, D.C.: GAO/GGD-90-57 (February 1990).

U.S. General Accounting Office. "Female Offenders: Who Are They and What Are the Problems Confronting Them?" Washington, D.C. (1979).

U.S. General Accounting Office. Washington, D.C.: GAO/GGD-91-21 (February 1991), 33–44.

U.S. General Accounting Office. Washington, D.C.: B-244494 (October 1991).

U.S. General Accounting Office. Washington, D.C.: Prison Expansion Report GAO/GGD-92-75 (May 1992).

U.S. General Accounting Office. "Foster Care, Parental Drug Abuse Has Alarming Impact on Young Children." Washington, D.C.: GAO/HEHS-94-89 (April 1994).

USA Today. (1993), 15A.

_____. "Mideast Getting Bulk of Aid." (January 12, 1995), 4A.

_____. "White Voters Lash Back." Linda Chavez, (November 16, 1994), 13A.

Vedder, Clyde, and Dora Sommerville. The Delinquent Girl. Springfield, Ill.: Charles Thomas, 1970.

Vega, M., I. Silverman, and J. Accardi. "The Female Felon." In H. E. Allen and N. L. Beran, editors, Reform in Correction: Problems and Issues. New York: Praeger, 1977.

Violent Crimes Control and Law Enforcement Act of 1994 (the Crime Bill).

Visher, Christy. "Gender, Police Arrest Decisions, and Notion of Chivalry." Criminology: An Interdisciplinary Journal 21 no. 1 (1983): 5–28.

Vital Statistics in Corrections. Laurel, Md.: American Correctional Association, 1980, 1985.

_____. College Park, Md.: American Correctional Association, 1988, 1989, 1990.

Voices of Triumph. "Perseverance." Alexandria, Va.: Time-Life Books, 1993.

Von Hentig, Hans. "The Criminality of Colored Women." University of Colorado Study Series 1, no. 3 (1942).

Ward, Bernie. Talk radio host. San Francisco, October 7, 1995.

Wallace, William. New York State Health Department Correspondence, February 8, 1995.

Weiss, J. "Liberation and Crime: The Invention of the New Criminal." Journal of Criminal Justice 6 (1976): 17–27

Welch, Susan, Michael Combs, and John Gruhl. "Do Black Judges Make a Difference?" American Sociological Review 46 (1988): 126–136.

Weller, Sheila. "Taking the Law Into Her Own Hands." *Redbook* (June 1992), 94–104.

Wingfield, Perry. "The Forgotten Victim: Report on the Families of Prisoners." *Corrections* 1 (Fall 1993).

Wise, Danell. "OCA Predicts System Will Manage with Fewer Judges." *New York Law Journal* (December 7, 1994), 1, col. 3.

Wyrich, E., S. Owens and O. Holloway. "Black Women, Income, and Incarceration." In C. E. Owens and J. Bell, eds., *Blacks and Criminal Justice*. Lexington, Mass.: D. C. Heath, 1977.

Index

150 Index

ILDS

Intersystems Library Delivery Services
Routing Labels

Do not remove this label until item reaches its destination

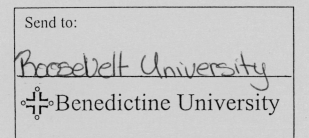

Send to:

Roosevelt University

⊹ Benedictine University

Circle destination library's ILDS address:

ALS-4	LCLS-5	SHLS-5
Augustana-4	Loyola U-1B	SIUC-6
Bradley U-3	LTLS-3	SIUE-5
Chicago PL-1A	MLS 1-A	SIUM-3
DePaul U- 1B	Neastern U-1B	SWIC-6
DLS-1A	Northern IL U-1A	U of Chicago- 1B
Eastern IL U- 3	NSLS-1B	UI Peoria- 3
Elmhurst Col- 1B	Nwestern U-1B	UI Rockford-1A
Gov State U-2	PALS CVLY-4	UI Urbana-3
IL Inst Tech-1B	PALS RKFD-1A	UIC-LHS-2
IL State Lib-3	PALS SHWD-1A	UIC Main Lib-2
ISU-3	Rte Cntrl Ofc-2	UIS-5
IL Wesleyan-3	(Roosevelt U-1B)	Wheaton Col-1B
Kankakee CC-2	RPLS-3	Western IL U-4

Notes: